On the Life, Writings, and Genius of Akenside:
by Charles Bucke

Address:
HardPress
8345 NW 66TH ST #2561
MIAMI FL 33166-2626
USA
Email: info@hardpress.net

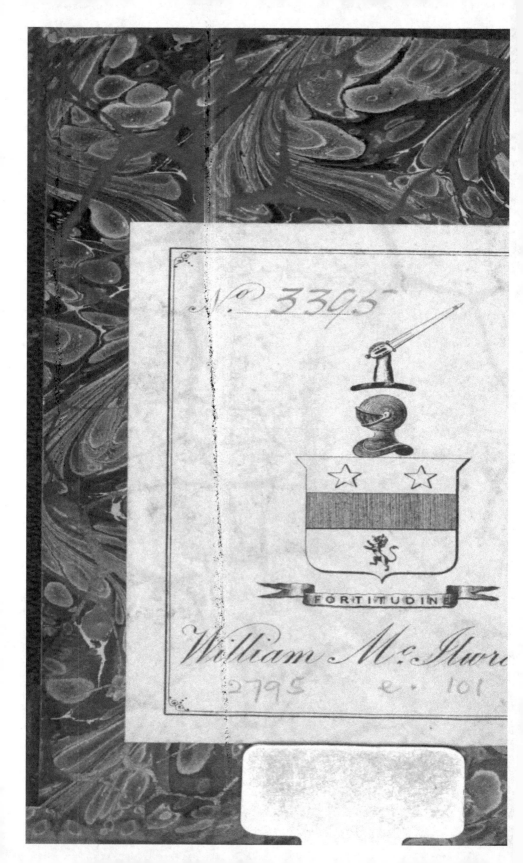

ON THE

LIFE, WRITINGS, AND GENIUS

OF

AKENSIDE:

WITH

SOME ACCOUNT OF HIS FRIENDS.

BY CHARLES BUCKE,

AUTHOR OF THE BEAUTIES, HARMONIES, AND SUBLIMITIES OF
NATURE.

—————————————— " The spacious west,
And all the teeming regions of the south,
Hold not a quarry to the curious flight
Of knowledge, half so tempting and so fair
As MAN to MAN."
Pleasures of Imagination.

LONDON:
JAMES COCHRANE AND CO., WATERLOO-PLACE.
1832

HAVING always esteemed the PLEASURES OF IMAGINATION the finest didactic Poem in our language, it was with no small pleasure, that I accidentally discovered, some time since, a few MS. notes of AKENSIDE at the British Museum.

These notes are not very important; but they led me to regret,—as, indeed, I had often done before,—that all the accounts, we have, of this great poet, should be so meagre and deficient :—and having formerly known two gentlemen, who had been intimately acquainted with him, I combined what I had heard them say of him with what was already known ; and taking his works for a general guide—(and few speak more in their works than Akenside does)—I have, I hope, been enabled to give a correct and, perhaps, not altogether an uninteresting outline of a virtuous and high-minded man, gifted with very considerable poetical powers.

The Reader will not expect me to give more than it was possible to obtain. I hope, he will rather thank me for what little I have been able to collect of this eminent person; though I cannot but feel, that he must greatly regret, that the subject did not fall into abler hands.

London.
January, 1832.

LIFE, WRITINGS, AND GENIUS

OF

AKENSIDE.

MARK AKENSIDE * was born at Newcastle-upon-Tyne, in the county of Northumberland, on the 9th of November, 1721. His father was a respectable butcher. His mother's name was Mary Lumsden. They were both exceedingly strict in their religious observances; and being in the habit of attending a meeting-house, which had been then recently erected in Hanover-square, their son was

* In all the editions of this poet, since the sixth published by Dodsley, 1763, the name has been invariably spelt AKENSIDE; but in the first edition of the Ode to the Earl of Huntingdon, the orthography is *Akinside,* and the poet himself, in his MS. dedication to Mr. Dyson (now first published) subscribes his name in the same manner.

B

baptized by the minister, (the Rev. Benjamin Bennet,) about three weeks afterwards.

Akenside is said to have been, in after life, very
much ashamed of the comparative lowness of his
birth ; and it is, also, reported, that he could never
regard a lameness, which impeded his walking with
facility, otherwise than as an unpleasant memento
of a cut on the foot, which he received from the
fall of one of his father's cleavers, when about seven
years of age.

Be this as it may, it is very certain that he had
a strong regard for the place of his birth ;—and
even so late as the year in which he died, (1770)
he wrote some beautiful lines, commemorative of
the pleasure, he was accustomed to receive, in early
life, from wandering among the scenes of his native
river.

> ——————————— " O ye dales
> Of *Tyne*, and ye, most ancient woodlands ! where
> Oft, as the giant flood obliquely strides,
> And his banks open, and his lawns extend,
> Stops short the pleased traveller to view,
> Presiding o'er the scene, some rustic tow'r,
> Founded by NORMAN or by SAXON hands."

No accounts have reached us, as to the number
of brothers and sisters he had : we only know,

from Brand's Observations on Popular Antiquities, that he knew one of Akenside's sisters, whose name was Addison, then living in Newcastle; and that she possessed several drawings, her brother had sketched at a very early period of life.

His parents having separated from the church, Akenside, after some preparatory instruction at the free-school of Newcastle, was placed under the care of a dissenting minister,—Mr. Wilson,—who kept a private academy in the same town; by whom his mind was early awakened to those impressions, which seldom fail—

" To render Nature pleasing to the eye,
  And music to the ear * ;—"

And that he was as feelingly alive to that most delightful of all suffrages,—the applause of the wise and good,—is evident from his Ode on the Love of Praise; than which Horace himself has scarcely one more beautiful.

I.
" Of all the springs within the mind,
    Which prompt her steps in Fortune's maze,
  From none more pleasing aid we find,
    Than from the genuine love of praise.

---

* Pleasures of Imagination, b. iii. 492.

II.

Nor any partial private end
    Such reverence to the public bears,
Nor any passion, Virtue's friend,
    So like to Virtue's self appears.

III.

For who in glory can delight,
    Without delight in virtuous deeds?
What man a charming voice can slight,
    Who courts the echo that succeeds?

IV.

But not the echo or the voice
    More, than on virtue, praise depends ;
To which, of course, its real price
    The judgment of the praiser tends.

V.

If praise, then, with religious awe
    From the sole perfect Judge be sought,
A nobler aim, a purer law,
    Nor priest, nor bard, nor sage hath taught

VI.

With which in character the same,
    Though in an humbler sphere it lies,
I count that soul of human fame
    The suffrage of the good und wise."

Thus, too, in his Ode on hearing a sermon preached against Glory :—

> " If to spurn at noble praise
>   Be the passport to thy heaven,
> Follow thou those gloomy ways ;
>   No such law to me was given.
>
>   Nor, I trust, shall I deplore me,
>   Faring like my friends before me,
>   Nor a holier place desire,
>   Than TIMOLEON's arms acquire,
> And TULLY's curule chair, and MILTON's golden lyre."

Akenside indulged his natural taste for poetry very early ; and, at the age of sixteen, sent to the editor of the Gentleman's Magazine a poem, written after the manner of Spenser, entitled the VIRTUOSO; the idea of which seems to have been taken from the subjoined passage of Shaftesbury's Characteristics *.

* " Hitherto there can lie no ridicule, nor the least scope for satiric wit or raillery. But when we push this virtuoso character a little further, and lead our polished gentleman into more nice researches ; when from the view of mankind and their affairs, our speculative genius, and minute examiner of nature's works, proceeds with equal or perhaps superior zeal, in the contemplation of the *insect life*, the conveniences, habitations, and economy of a race of *shell-fish;* when he has erected a *cabinet* in due form, and made it the real pattern of his mind, replete with the same trash and trumpery

This poem is not only curious, as a juvenile production, but as it serves to show how early the mind of Akenside was impregnated with the sentiments of that once celebrated writer.

Akenside did not think proper to republish this poem in the collection of his works ; and yet, there is not one stanza, of which he needed to have been, in the slightest degree, ashamed. Indeed, it is a very remarkable poem for so young a person. I shall quote the first and last stanzas, with its motto from Persius :

——————— *Videmus*
Nugari solitos.

" Whilom by silver Thames' gentle stream,
   In London town there dwelt a subtile wight ;
A wight of mickle wealth, and mickle fame,
   Book-learn'd and quaint ; a VIRTUOSO hight.
Uncommon things and rare were his delight ;
   From musings deep his brain ne'er gotten ease ;
Nor ceasen he from study day or night ;
   Until (advancing onwards by degrees)
He knew whatever breeds on earth, on air, or seas."

   *   *   *   *   *

---

of correspondent empty notions and chimerical conceits ; he then, indeed, becomes the subject of sufficient *raillery,* and is made the *jest* of common conversations."—*Characteristics,* vol. iii. p. 156. *Ed.* 1737.

" The wight, whose brain this phantom's * power doth fill,
   On whom she doth, with constant care, attend,
Will for a dreadful giant take a mill +,
   Or a grand palace in a hogstye find ‡ ;
(From her dire influence ME *may Heav'n defend!)*
   All things with vitiated sight he spies ;
Neglects his family, forgets his friend ;
   Seeks painted trifles and fantastic toys ;
And eagerly pursues imaginary joys."

Akenside seems to have entertained a particular contempt for virtuosos ; for he again makes that order of character a subject for ridicule in the third book of his principal poem.

—————————— " Behold yon mystic form,
Bedeck'd with feathers, insects, weeds, and shells!
Not with intenser view, the Samian sage
Bent his fixt eye on heaven's intenser fires,
When first the order of that radiant scene
Swell'd his exulting thought, than this surveys
A muckworm's entrails, or a spider's fang."

In the same year (viz. 1737) Akenside published, in the same miscellany, a Rhapsody on the miseries of a Poet, born to a low estate. This poem, as a whole, is scarcely worthy of preservation ; but as

* Phantasy's.
+ Alluding to a passage in Don Quixote ; about this time translated into English.
‡ From a line in Machiavelli's Asino.

there are some passages, indicative of future excellence, I shall quote them.

> " Of all the various lots around the ball,
>   Which Fate to man distributes, absolute,
>   Avert, ye Gods ! 'that of the Muses' son,
>   Cursed with dire poverty,   Poor, hungry wretch !
>   What shall he do for life ? He cannot work
>   With manual labour.   Shall those sacred hands,
>   That brought the counsels of the Gods to light,
>   Shall that inspired tongue, which every muse
>   Has touched divine, to charm the sons of men,
>   These hallow'd orgies—these ! be prostitute
>   To the vile service of some fool in power,
>   All his behests submissive to perform,
>   Howe'er to him ungrateful ?   Oh ! he scorns
>   Th' ignoble thought !"

The following passage, no doubt, alludes to an order of persons, with whom the poet was, at this time, compelled occasionally to associate.

> " But 'tis in vain to rave at destiny.
>   Here he must rest ; and brook the best he can ;
>   To live remote from grandeur, learning, wit,
>   Immured among th' *ignoble, vulgar herd*
>   *Of lowest intellect ; whose stupid souls*
>   *But half inform their bodies.*"

The succeeding lines allude to the various descriptions of poetry, in a manner very appropriate and concise.

" Upon his brow
Perplex'd anxiety, and struggling thought,
Painful as female throes! *whether the bard*
Display the deeds of heroes ; or the fall
Of vice in lay dramatic; or expand
The lyric wing; or in elegiac strains
Lament the fair ; or lash the stubborn age
With laughing satire."

After depicting the miseries of the poet, left only to his own mental energies to sustain the loss of friends, the want of a Halifax, of a Somers, or of a Dorset, and the miseries of indigence, he closes the theme with a striking admonition to himself.

" I hear my better angel cry, ' *Retreat!*
Rash youth, in time retreat ! Let those poor bards,
Who slighted all,—all! for the flattering Muse,
Yet cursed with piercing want, *as land-marks stand,*
*To warn thee from the service of th' ingrate *.*'"

The next poem, he sent to the Gentleman's Magazine was a fable, illustrative of CONTENT and AMBITION ; and it is really not too much to say of it, that it is almost worthy of being associated with some of the translations which, a few years previous, had been rendered from Ovid's Metamorphoses.

* I found this passage inscribed in pencil on the wall of an inn at Cassel, in the department of the North, a few months ago. It was, no doubt, written by some unfortunate English votary of the Muses, then on his, perhaps, *compelled* travels.

He fables, that, in times—

> " While yet the world was young, and men were few,
>   Nor lurking fraud, nor tyrant rapine knew ;"

CONTENT was the only acknowledged sovereign of mankind.

> " Joy of all hearts, delight of every eye,
>   Nor grief, nor pain, appear'd, when she was by ;
>   Her presence from the wretched banish'd care,
>   Dispersed the swelling sigh, and stopt the falling tear."

At length, AMBITION

> ——————————— " hellish fiend ! arose
>   To plague the world, and banish man's repose."

This fiend, determining on the dethronement of CONTENT, all the vain, and lovers of novelty, flocked to his standard : CONTENT was, in consequence, dethroned, and compelled to wander about the world in search of a home.

One day, forsaken by every one, and destitute of all things, she came to a cottage, roofed with turf.

> " Fast by a gloomy, venerable wood
>   Of shady pines, and ancient oaks, it stood."

In this retired cottage, bending beneath a weight of years, a cheerful couple

> ——————————— " had pass'd their life.
> The husband INDUSTRY was call'd—FRUGALITY the wife."

This pair had many sons, whose occupation consisted in cultivating the earth. They had also one daughter, whose name was PLENTY.

In former years, CONTENT had occasionally visited this cottage; and being now stripped of her dominions, she determined on seeking in it a refuge from her misfortunes.

> " Arrived,—she makes her changed condition known;
> Tells how the rebels drove her from the throne;"

and implores shelter from the TYRANT. The aged pair listened in sympathy to her misfortunes, invited her into their cottage, and entreated her to take up her abode in the bosom of their family.

In the meantime, AMBITION having attained the summit of his wishes,

> " Polluted every stream with human gore,
> And scatter'd plagues and death from shore to shore."

Offended at the evils thus entailed upon mankind, JUPITER looked down with indignation and pity. He desires VENUS to dispatch her son, CUPID, to repair to the palace of AMBITION, and to strike him with an ardent love for his former rival, CONTENT. Then he commanded MERCURY to descend to the regions of PLUTO,

> " To rouse OBLIVION from her sable cave;"

and enjoins her to draw around the abode of CON-
TENT, a darkness equal to the

     ——————————— " ' deepest gloom of night,
    To screen the VIRGIN from the TYRANT's sight;
    That the vain purpose of his life may try,
    Still to explore, what still eludes his eye.'
    He spake:—Loud praises shake the bright abode,
    And all applaud the justice of the god."

This poem, and several others, Akenside did not
feel ambitious of acknowledging; and they are introduced here, not with an intention of advancing
his reputation, but as specimens of the poetical
power, he possessed, at an early period of life.

But though Akenside did not choose to associate
them with the fruit of his maturer years, he occasionally alludes, and always with satisfaction, to the
time in which they were written.   Thus in his
ode to his Muse, written many years after:

   " And now again my bosom burns;
    The Muse, the Muse herself, returns!
    Such on the banks of TYNE, confest,
    I hail'd the fair immortal guest,
    When first she seal'd me for her own,
    Made all her blissful treasures known,
    And bade me swear to follow her alone."

Some of his productions, however, at this period, seem to have touched on subjects, which he did not, afterwards, approve; at least, so we may conjecture from a passage in his second poem on the Pleasures of Imagination.

——————————— " What though first
In years unseason'd,—haply ere the sports
Of childhood yet were o'er,—th' adventurous lay,
With many splendid prospects, many charms,
Allured my heart; not conscious whence they sprung,
Nor heedful of their end? yet serious truth
Her empire o'er the calm sequester'd theme
Asserted soon; while falsehood's evil brood,
Vile and deceitful pleasure, she at once
Excluded: and my fancy's careless toil
Drew to the better cause."

While still a boy, he often, as we have before observed, amused his leisure from the duties of education, by wandering on the banks of the Tyne, where he hailed the morning and evening sun with all the enthusiasm of youth, and felt the impress of poetical inspiration. He frequently alludes to these moments of delight.

——————————— " Pierian maids!
Hear me propitious. In the morn of life,
When Hope shone bright, and all the prospect smiled,

To your sequester'd mansion, oft my steps
Were turn'd, O Muses! and within your gate
My offerings paid."

P. I. Second Poem, iii. 345.

Again, in his hymn to the Naiads :—

" The Muses (sacred by their gifts divine),
In early days did to my wondering sense
Their secrets oft reveal:—oft my raised ear
In slumber felt their music ; oft at noon,
Or hour of sunset, by some lonely stream,
In field or shady grove, they taught me words
Of power from death and envy to preserve
The good man's name."

About the age of seventeen he was frequently at the house of a relative, at Morpeth ; and to the enjoyments he there experienced, in studying the works of Nature, he alludes in lines, perhaps, from their associations, the most beautiful to himself, in all his poems.

" O ye Northumbrian shades! which overlook
The rocky pavement and the mossy falls
Of solitary WENSBECK's limpid stream,
How gladly I recall your well-known seats,
Beloved of old ; and that delightful time,
When all alone, for many a summer's day,
I wander'd through your calm recesses; led
In silence, by some powerful hand unseen."

P. I. Second Poem, iv. l. 38.

Many poets have recorded the beauties of their native stream ; and Armstrong, in a poem published in the same year with that of Akenside, followed the example.

> ———————————— " Such the stream,
> On whose Arcadian banks, I first drew air,
> LIDDAL; till now in Doric lays
> Tuned to her murmurs by her love-sick swains,
> Unknown in song:—though not a purer stream
> Through meads more flow'ry, more romantic groves,
> Rolls towards the western main."

While at Morpeth, Akenside is supposed by some to have written his Pleasures of Imagination. But this is scarcely to be credited ; though it is not improbable, that many passages may have been written there. His portrait of Dione, for instance.

> ——————— " O bear, then, unreproved,
> Thy smiling treasures to the green recess,
> Where young DIONE strays ; with sweetest airs
> Entice her forth, to lend her angel form
> For beauty's honor'd image."

At the age of eighteen Akenside was sent to Edinburgh, with a view of taking orders as a dissenting minister. In this resolution he remained one year ; when he altered his intention in respect to the choice of a profession, and entered himself as a student in medicine. The money, therefore, he had received from the Dissenters' Society, and which it was customary for them to appropriate to the education of young men of scanty fortune, designed for their ministry, he afterwards returned.

He remained at Edinburgh as a medical student two years, during which period he seems to have made great progress. He was elected a member of the Medical Society, was greatly respected for his attainments, and became acquainted with several young men, who afterwards distinguished themselves in a very eminent manner; amongst whom we may particularly mention Dr. John Gregory and Dr. Robertson. And here we may with advantage introduce a curious anecdote, related by Dr. Stewart, in his Elements of the Principles of the Human Mind *. "There are various passages in Akenside's works," says he, "which will be read with additional pleasure, when it is known, that they were not entirely suggested by fancy. I allude to those passages where he betrays a secret consciousness of powers, adapted to a higher station of life than fell to his lot. Akenside, when a medical student at

* Vol. iii. p. 501. 4to.

Edinburgh, was a member of the Medical Society, then recently formed, and was eminently distinguished by the eloquence which he displayed in the course of the debates. Dr. Robertson (who was at that time a student of divinity in the same university) told me, that he was frequently led to attend their meetings, chiefly to hear the speeches of Akenside; the great object of whose ambition then was a seat in Parliament; a situation which, he was sanguine enough to flatter himself, he had some prospect of obtaining, and for which he conceived his talents to be much better adapted than for the profession he had chosen."

What the circumstances were, which could justify the ambition of Akenside, it is now too late to inquire. Perhaps it was merely a sally, arising out of a consciousness of oratorical power, and which power he possessed to the last year of his life; but to this hope Dr. Stewart supposes he alludes in one of the stanzas in his Ode to Sleep.

> " Nor yet those awful forms present
> For chiefs and heroes only meant.
> The figured brass, the choral song,
> The rescued people's glad applause,
> The listening senate, and the laws
> Fix'd by the counsels of TIMOLEON's tongue,

C

> Are scenes too grand for Fortune's private ways:
> And though they shine in youth's ingenuous view,
> The sober, gainful arts of modern days
> To such romantic thoughts have bad a long adieu."
>
> *Stanza 4.*

The scene had altered; experience had stept in; the world had taught him a lesson; and the more sober ambition had visited his imagination of desiring such dreams, as those, which animated the eyelids of Mead and Milton.

> " But Morpheus ! on thy balmy wing
> Such honourable visions bring,
> As soothed great MILTON's injured age ;
> When in prophetic dreams he saw
> The race, unborn, with pious awe
> Imbibe each virtue from his heavenly page;
> Or such as MEAD's benignant fancy knows,
> When health's deep treasures, by his art explored,
> Have saved the infant from an orphan's woes,
> Or to his trembling sire his age's hope restored."

In the year, previous to his journey to Edinburgh, Akenside wrote a poem, entitled a *British Philippick;* a satire, occasioned by the preparations for the war, which were then making, in consequence of the insults, the country had received from Spain. This poem is remarkable for little, if we except the spirit of patriotism in which it was composed.

During his residence at Edinburgh, he is, also, supposed to have written his Hymn to Science, and an Ode on the Winter Solstice. The Hymn to Science was not inserted in any collection of his poems till 1793. The cause of this omission I have not been able to discover. The hymn itself is so far from being unworthy the genius of its author, that it is not a praise too unmeasured to assert, that it is even worthy the lyre of Collins. The 12th and 13th stanzas are particularly beautiful.

> " That last best effort of thy skill,
>   To form the life and rule the will,
>   Propitious Pow'r ! impart :
>   Teach me to cool my passion's fires,
>   Make me the judge of my desires,
>   The master of my heart.
>
> Raise me above the vulgar's breath,
> Pursuit of fortune, fear of death,
>   And all in life that's mean ;
> Still true to reason be my plan,
> Still let my actions speak the man,
>   Through every various scene."

Has Horace or Gray any thing superior to this ?

The Ode on the Winter Solstice he soon after improved into another ode ; both of which are ge-

c 2

nerally printed in succession. There are fine passages in both; but the second is, I think, far superior to the first. The late Miss Seward of Lichfield says, in one of her letters, that she regularly read it every winter.

Some have supposed this ode to have been written in Holland; but the following stanza seems to justify those, who believe it to have been written in Scotland.

> " But lo! on this deserted coast,
>   How faint the light, how chill the air!
> Lo! arm'd with whirlwind, hail, and frost,
>   Fierce Winter desolates the year,
> The fields resign their cheerful bloom,
> No more the breezes breathe perfume;
> No more the warbling waters roll;
>   Desarts of snow fatigue the eye;
>   Successive tempests bloat the sky,
> And gloomy damps oppress the soul."

There are some fine passages in this ode; but it cannot be denied, that, in pathos and sublimity, it is much inferior to the Dirge of BURNS; written, I have somewhere read, one evening after perusing the ode by Akenside:

> " The wintry west extends his blast,
>   An' hail an' rain does blaw;
> Or the stormy north sends drivin forth
>   The blindin sleet an' snaw:

While tumblin brown, the burn comes down,
  An' roars frae bank to brae;
An' bird an' beast in covert rest,
  An' pass the heartless day.

' The sweeping blast, the sky o'ercast *,'
  The joyless winter-day,
Let others fear;—to me more dear
  Than a' the pride o' May.
The tempest's howl; it soothes my soul;
  My griefs it seems to join:
The leafless trees my fancy please;
  Their fate resembles mine.

Thou Pow'r Supreme! whose mighty scheme
  These woes of mine fulfil;
Here, firm, I rest; they *must* be best,
  Because they are thy will!
Then all I want (O do thou grant
  This one request of mine!)
Since to *enjoy* thou dost deny,
  Assist me to resign."

After a stay of three years, Akenside removed
to Leyden, in farther pursuit of medical knowledge;
and there had the good fortune to form a strict and
never-sleeping friendship with a young man of
family and fortune, who was prosecuting the study
of civil law in that university. This gentleman's
name was DYSON; and to him Akenside was indebted for most of his subsequent ease in life.

* Dr. Young.

At Leyden he began, if I mistake not, to me-
thodize the great poem, he had begun; and it is
probable that he communicated the manuscript to
his new friend, Mr. Dyson; from whom he had
the benefit of receiving advice, unbiassed by any
desire of being esteemed a critic;—an inestimable
advantage to any one engaged in high designs,
whether in literature, legislation, or politics.   This,
I think, is evident from the following passage:—

——————" Nor to truth's recess divine,
Through this wide argument's unbeaten space,
Withholding surer guidance; while, by turns,
We traced the sages old, or while the queen
Of Sciences (whom manners and the mind
Acknowledge) to my true companion's voice,
Not unattentive, o'er the wintry lamp
Inclined her sceptre favouring."
P. I. second Poem, i. l. 62.

At Leyden, too, he may be supposed to have
written his HYMN to CHEERFULNESS, the most popular of all his minor poems:—in reading which
we cannot refuse to accede to the opinion of Hume,
that a cheerful disposition is worth ten thousand a
year.   In no part of his works is the poet seen to
more advantage; and it is impossible to read it
without imbibing a belief, that he was,—when neither insulted or otherwise ill-used,—the kindest

friend and most favourably disposed to administer to the happiness of others, of all human beings. The following passage reminds us of the grand moral of the Pleasures of Imagination.

> " O thou ! whose pleasing pow'r I sing,
> Thy lenient influence hither bring,
> Compose the storm, dispel the gloom,
> Till Nature wears her wonted bloom,
> Till fields and shades their sweets exhale,
> And music swell each op'ning gale !
> Then o'er his breast thy softness pour,
> And let him learn the timely hour,
> To trace the world's benignant laws,
> And judge of the presiding cause;
> Who founds on discord Beauty's reign,
> Converts to pleasure every pain,
> Subdues each hostile form to rest,
> And bids the universe be blest."

After remaining three years at Leyden, Akenside was admitted to the degree of doctor of physic, (May 16, 1744) ; and in conformity to the custom of Dutch universities, published a thesis on the original and growth of the Human Fœtus ; a dissertation which gained him great credit * ; as the opinion, he suggested, departed in many particulars from the one then received, and has been the one almost universally acted upon since.

* Johnson.

Previous to leaving Leyden he bade farewell to a country

> " Which Pan, which Ceres never knew,
> Nor ever mountain zephyr blew,"

in an ode, the best stanzas of which are those, in which he celebrates his native country.

Having completed the relative objects of their voyage to Holland, the two friends, Dyson and Akenside, embarked in the same vessel at Rotterdam, and arrived safely in London, after an agreeable but protracted voyage. On their arrival, the one took to the bar, and became a constitutional lawyer; the other, of course, resorted to physic. This contrast of occupation is elegantly touched upon in the second poem on the Pleasures of Imagination.

> —————————————" Now the Fates
> Have other tasks imposed. To thee, my friend !
> The ministry of Freedom, and the faith
> Of popular decrees in early youth,
> Not vainly they committed. Me they sent
> To wait on pain, and silent arts to urge
> Inglorious, not ignoble ; if my cares,
> To such as languish on a grievous bed,
> Ease, and the sweet forgetfulness of ill
> Conciliate ;—nor delightless, if the Muse
> Her shades to visit, and to taste her springs,—

If some distinguish'd hours the bounteous Muse
Impart, and grant (what she and she alone
Can grant to mortals), that my hand those wreaths
Of fame, and honest favour, which the bless'd
Wear in Elysium, and which never felt
The breath of envy or malignant tongues,
That *these* my hand for thee and for myself
May gather."

P. I. Second Poem, i. 68.

The Pleasures of Imagination. being completed, Akenside sought the earliest opportunity of publishing it. It was sent, in consequence, to Dodsley, with a demand of one hundred and twenty pounds for the copyright. This demand, we are told, being higher than Dodsley chose to give hastily, he carried the manuscript to Pope, and requested advice. Pope looked into it, says Johnson (who had his information from Dodsley himself), and perceiving its merit, told him " to make no niggardly offer," since " this was no every day writer."

Dodsley immediately closed with the author; and the manuscript was placed in the hands of Richardson, the celebrated author of Pamela, Sir Charles Grandison, and Clarissa Harlowe, to print; and here, though written some years after, we may introduce one of the few letters, which remain of this elegant poet. It is still preserved in manuscript, among the papers of Dr. Birch, at the British Museum ; and though containing no information of importance, yet to those, not accustomed to matters, relative to errors of the press, it may serve to show the anxiety of an author, when he discovers any error, too late to be rectified.

" *To Mr. Richardson, in Salisbury-court, Fleet-street.*

" Sir—I return you many thanks for sending me the sheet, about which I wrote to you.   I find in it an *erratum*, and of that unlucky sort, which does not make absolute nonsense, but only conveys a false and absurd idea.   The sheet is marked T t ; and in page 328 and line ninth from the bottom, *stream* is printed instead of *steam.*   If you can, without much trouble, print this as an erratum, or rather let some one with a stroke of a pen blot out the *r*, as the sheets are dried, I should be greatly obliged.

" I am, Sir, with true respect,
" Your most humble servant,
" M. Akenside.
" *Bloomsbury Square, Jan. 25.*"

The poem being suited chiefly for the highest order of readers, it is not a little surprising, that it should have arrived, at once, at the zenith of a fame, from which, like most other works popular in their day, it has never declined. All readers, however, were not satisfied; and, among the rest, GRAY. For when Dr. Wharton, of Old Park, near Durham, wrote to him, a few weeks after the publication, in what manner it was esteemed at Cambridge, Gray, in a hasty reply *, told him, that he wondered, he should ask an opinion, as to what the Cambridge men thought, since many of them, who pretended to judge things, did not judge at all; and those, who were wiser, gave no judgment, till they heard those pronounced by the frequenters of Dick's and the Rainbow Coffee-houses. " However," continued he, " to show you, that I am a judge, as well as my countrymen, I will tell you; though I have rather turned it over than read it (but no matter; no more have they), that it seems to me above the middling; and now and then, for a little while, rises even to the best, particularly in description. It is often obscure, and even unintelligible; and too much infected with the Hutchinsonian jargon. In short, its great fault is, that it was published at least nine years too early;

* Dated April 26, 1744.

and so, methinks, in a few words, à la mode du Temple, I have very pertly dispatched what, perhaps, may for several years have employed a very ingenious man, worthy fifty of myself."

That Akenside occupied a rank, below Gray as a lyric poet, (though his ode to the Earl of Huntingdon would place him on the same elevation in the opinion of many), is, I think, not safely to be doubted: but that he had a more brilliant imagination, a truer impulse, a finer touch of musical expression, and a more exquisite sense of nature on the lofty impulses of mind is, I think, as little to be denied; since the poetical merit of Gray (always excepting his unequalled Elegy), seems to have consisted chiefly in a mature wisdom of selection, and a masterly arrangement of other men's ideas: that is, he knew diamonds, when he saw them in the quarry; he knew equally well how to polish them; and he had an equal judgment in setting them to the best advantage. No one of his age, therefore, had a mind, more capable of appreciating Akenside, than he had. I, therefore, think it more than probable, that when he read the Pleasures of Imagination with greater attention, than merely " turning over the leaves" (since Akenside is not to be appreciated but after a third reading), this accomplished critic, as well as poet, must have altered his opinion; and I think (but of that I am not quite certain), that the late Mr. Meyrick told me as much. Be this, however, as it may, it is very certain, that the poem rose into immediate estimation; and has ever since been considered by most competent judges, one of the finest and most classical productions in our language.

Mr. Meyrick, whom I have just now mentioned, was a very remarkable person. He was a surgeon and apothecary, retired from business, and past eighty when I first knew him; yet he had all the hilarity of youth. He knew, at least he had seen, all the eminent literary characters of the time in which he lived; and was full of anecdote, more particularly in respect to their distresses. He frequently called in Akenside; whom he visited as a friend, and recommended as a physician. "We were not very much like either," said the old gentleman; "for he was stiff and set; and I all life and spirits. He often frowned upon me in a sick room. He could not bear to see any one smile in the presence of an invalid; and, I think, he lost a good deal of business by the solemn sententiousness of his air and manner. I wanted to cheer patients up!" Mr. Meyrick knew ARMSTRONG, also, the author of the Art of Preserving Health. "He ruined himself," said he, " by that foolish performance of his, the Economy of Love. How, in the name of heaven, could he ever expect that a woman would let him enter her house again, after that? The man was a fool! He, who undertakes to be a physician, must be chastity itself."

Akenside and Armstrong published their principal poems in the same year. They appealed to the consent of mankind in opposite directions. For if the poem on the PLEASURES OF IMAGINATION is rich in materials, and brilliant in imagery and versification, the ART OF PRESERVING HEALTH is as remarkable for its simplicity of style, and a total rejection of ornament. Their success as poets is said to have equally retarded their success as physicians. They associated occasionally; but their characters never assimilated. Akenside was solemn in manner, but engaging and polite; except when unwarrantably put upon, when he became irritable, though never overbearing. Armstrong relapsed into a morbid sensibility, the languid listlessness of which is said to have damped the vigour of his intellectual efforts to that degree, that some have even ventured to suppose, that he sat for the following picture in Thomson's Castle of Indolence.

" With him was sometimes join'd in silent walk,
   (Profoundly silent, for they never spoke)
   One shyer still, who quite detested talk ;
   If stung by spleen, at once away he broke
   To groves of pine, and broad o'ershadowing oak :
   There, inly thrill'd, he wander'd all alone,
   And on himself his pensive fury wroke ;
   He never utter'd word, save when first shone
The glittering star of eve—' Thank heaven! the day is done!'"

When Thomson's Castle of Indolence appeared, Akenside was in raptures with it. Mr. Meyrick had his copy. Many stanzas were marked very emphatically ; among the rest the following—

" I care not, fortune, what you me deny :
   You cannot rob me of free nature's grace ;
   You cannot shut the windows of the sky,
   Through which Aurora shews her bright'ning face ;
   You cannot bar my constant feet to trace
   The woods and lawns by living streams at eve."

Akenside's poem was published anonymously. There was, therefore, no dedication ; but the following still exists in MS., prefixed to the first edition in quarto, which the poet presented to Mr.

Dyson, whose modesty, I suppose, would not permit it to appear.

VIRO CONJUNCTISSIMO
JEREMIÆ DYSON,
VITÆ, MORUMQUE SUORUM DUCI,
RERUM BONARUM SOCIO,
STUDIORUM JUDICI,
CUJUS AMICITIA
NEQUE SANCTIUS HABET QUICQUAM,
NEQUE OPTAT CARIUS;
HOCCE OPUSCULUM
(VOS, Ô TYRANNORUM IMPURA LAUDES
ET SERVILIUM BLANDIMENTA POETARUM,
ABESTE PROCUI)
DAT, DICAT, CONSECRATQUE
MARCUS AKINSIDE,
xvii Calendas Jan. A. Æ. C. MDCCXLIV.

Some few years after the publication of this poem, it was translated into French, and afterwards into Italian. The French translation having been rendered in prose * can, of course, give French readers

* This translation was first published, anonymously, at Amsterdam in 1759, prefaced in the following manner.

" *Ce pöeme parut, en Angleterre pour la première fois en 1744; il y fut reçu avec très grands applaudissements; l'on en a fait depuis un grand nombre d'éditions, on a cru que l'on en verroit avec plaisir la traduction en François; rien n'a été omis pour qu'elle fût exacte, cependant on seul*

but a very imperfect idea of a poem, one chief excellence of which consists in the splendour of its versification. The translator was Baron d'Holbach, a Member of the Academies of St. Petersburg, Manheim, and Berlin, who died at Paris in 1789; after enjoying the friendships of Helvetius, Diderot, d'Alembert, Marmontel, Condillac, Turgot, Buffon, and Rousseau. He was author of many works on mineralogy, chemistry, and natural history.

The translation into Italian is by the ABBATE ANGELO MAZZA. This translation is a very scarce

sent que la prose ne peut rendre que foiblement les beautés de la poësie. Un sujet tel que les Plaisirs de l'Imagination, demandoit à être traité avec chaleur et enthousiasme; l'on n'aura rien à reprocher a l'auteur de ce côté là. L'ivresse poétique et l'espece de désordre qui regnent dans son ouvrage, sembleroient même convenir plutôt à une ode qu'à un Poëme Epique; ce qui a fait dire plaisamment à Milord Chesterfield, que ce livre étoit le plus beau de ceux qu'il n'entendoit pas. Cependant pour peu qu'on y fasse attention, on trouvera que cet air de désordre est peut-être un effet de l'art, et sert à couvrir une liaison plus grande que le premier coup d'œil n'en promettoit. Le choix des comparaisons, la noblesse des peintures, la pompe des expressions que l'auteur, a répandues à pleines mains dans son poëme, sont de nature à plaire à toutes les personnes qui auront de la sensibilité et du goût; la philosophie, parée des ornemens des arts, en devient plus propre à exercer son empire sur les hommes."

D

book in this country.   The only copy, I have been
able to procure a sight of, is that in the library of
George the Third, presented to the British Museum,
by his late Majesty, George the Fourth.   Specimens will be given in several subsequent pages.

MAZZA was born at Parma, Nov. 21, 1740; but
he was educated at Reggio.   He went afterwards
to Padua, and thence to Venice ; where he produced
his translation.   In 1768 he was called to the chair
of Greek Literature at Parma.   He subsequently
removed to Bologna, where he published a translation of Pindar's Odes: soon after which he was
admitted into the Arcadian Academy at Rome.   He
died in 1817.

The subject matter of Akenside's poem is so
strikingly condensed, that it must ever be a work
of great difficulty to a translator.   We ought not,
therefore, to be surprised at the diffuseness of
Mazza's translation ; the aggregate of which may
be shown by the number of lines in each.

Original Poem.		Italian Translation.
Book I.	604 lines.	764 lines.
II.	771	944
III.	633	783
	2008	2491

The Pleasures of the Imagination was published with the following passage (as a motto), from Epictetus apud Arrian, ii. 23.

Ασεβὲς μὲν ἐστιν ἀνθρώπῳ τὰς παρὰ τῷ Θεῷ χάριτας ἀτιμαξειν.

The poem having been published anonymously, a person named ROLT, an author of some vanity and pretension, went, it is said, to Dublin, and there published an edition of it in his own name; on the fame of which he lived for several months. Boswell, who gives this anecdote in his life of Johnson, says, that Akenside, being informed of this, " vindicated his right, by publishing the poem with its real author's name." In a note, however, the biographer states, " I have made inquiry in Ireland as to this story; but I do not find it recollected there. I give it on the authority of Dr. Johnson; to which may be added the Biographical Dictionary, and the Biographia Dramatica; in both of which it has stood many years. Mr. Malone observes, that the truth, probably, is, that an edition was not published with Rolt's name in the title-page; but that the poem being anonymous,

Rolt acquiesced in its being attributed to him in conversation*."

Shortly after the publication of this poem, Akenside published a never-dying satire on Mr. Pulteney; who, from being idolized as the best and firmest patriot of his age, suddenly sacrificed all his popularity for the vulgar consideration of an empty title†, without office, without influence, or the least substantial advantage. "Doubtless," says the historian‡, " he flattered himself with the hope of one day directing the councils of his sovereign; but this was never accomplished;

---

* Rolt was engaged in many literary undertakings, none of which are now remembered. Churchill, however, mentions him in the Rosciad.

" Secret as night, with ROLT's experienced aid,
　The plan of future operations laid."

He was author of

ELIZA, a musical entertainment, set to music by Dr. Arne.

ALMENA, an opera, set to music by Dr. Arne. The story is from the Persian.

The ROYAL SHEPHERD; an opera, from Metastasio, who formed his plot on a passage in Quintus Curtius. Lib. iv. c. 3, 4.

† The Earldom of Bath. 　　　‡ Smollett, xix. 79.

and he remained a solitary monument of blasted ambition."

The indignation of the public, at the weakness of Mr. Pulteney, was almost beyond precedent; Akenside partook of it; and, in consequence, in an epistle to Curio, did not hesitate to stigmatize the disgraced patriot as the betrayer of his country.

This epistle he afterwards altered into an ode; and both are generally printed in a collection of his poems; but the original far transcends the copy. There are, in the ode, some fine lines; but Johnson, as he frequently does, speaks idly, when he pronounces it to be disgraceful only to the author.

The following passage from Cicero was prefixed to it, by way of motto: " *Neque tam ulciscendi causa dixi, quam ut et in præsens sceleratos cives timore ab impugnanda patria detinerem; et in posterum, documentum statuerem, nequis talem amentiam vellet imitari.*"

In the mean time, the fame of his great poem spread widely among persons of taste; but some observations having appeared in one of the notes, in conformity to Shaftesbury's opinion, that ridicule is the test of truth, WARBURTON thought proper to make some severe strictures on that opinion, in a postscript, prefixed to a new edition of that stupendous monument of misapplied learning—the Divine Legation of Moses.

In this postscript Warburton classed Akenside, as a poet, in the same rank with Lord Kaimes (who in his Elements of Criticism had espoused the same argument *), as a critic. " The poet," says he, " is a follower of Lord Shaftesbury's fancies; the critic a follower of his own. Both men of taste, and equally anxious for the well-doing of ridicule."

This postscript gave great offence to Akenside; and his friend, Mr. Dyson, who seems to have understood the duties of friendship better than the canons of philosophy, armed in defence of him, and wrote an " *Epistle to the Rev. Mr. Warburton, occasioned by his treatment of the author of the Pleasures of Imagination.*" We may judge of the style of this letter by the following extract :

" Notwithstanding the pains you have taken to discourage men from entering into any controversy with you ; and notwithstanding the severe example you have just been making of one, who, as you fancied, had presumed to call you to account ; you must still be content to be accountable for your writings ; and must, once more, bear the mortification of being actually called to

* Part v. chap. vii. xii.

account for them. It is the preface to your late Remarks, that you are now called upon to justify; in which you have thought fit to treat upon a mighty free footing (as you style it, but in the apprehension of most people, upon a very injurious one), the ingenious and worthy author of the poem, entitled 'The Pleasures of Imagination.' The favourable reception and applause, that performance has met with, render it unnecessary, and indeed impertinent, for me to enlarge in its praise; especially as you, sir, have not condescended to enter into a particular censure of the poem. However, by some general hints, scattered up and down, as well as by the affectation of perpetually styling the author *our poet,* you have let us see how you stand affected towards it. Whether it be, indeed, that dull, trivial, useless thing, you seem to represent it, I shall not dispute with you; but am content to have, as to this point, Mr. Warburton's judgment staked against the general reputation of the poem. The point I am immediately concerned with, is, your unbecoming treatment of the author; which, as it is so interwoven through the whole course of your preface, as to be sufficiently evident without the allegation of repeated passages; so we shall find there are not wanting repeated instances of direct and notorious ill usage;—such usage as, though the provocation had been ever so just, and the imagined attack upon you ever so real, would have yet been unwarrantable; and which, therefore, cannot admit of the least shadow of an excuse, when it shall appear, that you had really no provocation at all."

To this letter Warburton never replied.

The indignation of Akenside, and the zeal of Mr. Dyson, were a little too unmeasured; for the critic did not attack Akenside as a man, nor as a poet; he merely designated him a follower of Lord Shaftesbury; and an apologist for an opinion, that has now long been given up as untenable. Indeed the argument is, in itself, a species of the ridiculous. For who employs ridicule so often as half-informed, half-witted, insolent, and conceited persons? If ridicule, therefore, is a test of truth, these half-informed, half-witted, insolent, and conceited persons are the best judges of the most serious and sacred things *.

---

* " Ridicule may befriend either truth or falsehood; and as it is morally or immorally applied, may illustrate the one, or disguise the other. Yet it should seem, that the moral is more natural, than the immoral application of ridicule; inasmuch as truth is more congenial to the mind than falsehood, and so, the real more easily made apparent, than the fictitious images of things. * * *

" Ridicule, therefore, being of a vague, unsteady nature, merely relative to the imaginations and passions of mankind, there must be several orders or degrees of it, suited to the fancies and capacities of those, whom the artist attempts to influence.

" But however ridicule may impress the idea of apparent turpitude or falsehood on the imagination; yet still reason

The subject of ridicule, indeed, is, in this poem, an intrusion; and that the author himself thought it so, may be inferred from his having, in the second poem, curtailed the subject so much, that what, in his first, occupies two hundred and seven lines, is reduced in the second to only fifty. The statement as to the final cause, however, is the same in both.

Akenside, I believe, was occasionally given to ridicule; and in return was himself ridiculed by a class of persons, with whom it was no great honour to be associated. Smollett did all he could against

remains the superior and corrective power. Therefore, every representation of ridicule, which only applies to the fancy and affections, must finally be examined and decided upon, must be tried, rejected, or received, as the reasoning faculty shall determine; and thus ridicule can never be a detector of falsehood, or a test of truth."—*Brown's Essays on the Characteristics of the Earl of Shaftesbury.*

See Characteristics, i. p. 30, 31, 61; also 11, 12, 128, 129.

For Warburton's opinion, see Divine Legation of Moses, vol. i. x. xviii. xxxvii. xxxix.

Horace sums up the power of ridicule in one of those concise periods, of which he was so great a master.

——————— Ridiculum acri
Fortius et melius magnas plerumque secat res.

The power of ridicule is admitted; but that power is very different from the test.

him in this way, in his novel of Peregrine Pickle; to which he is said to have been prompted by a pique *, he had taken, in consequence of Akenside's having made some reflections against Scotland.

We may here, perhaps, be excused for introducing a curious anecdote, in respect to Smollett. As he was one day going out of Paternoster-row up Warwick-lane leading to Warwick-square, a butcher came out of his slaughter-house with a dead sheep upon his back : " Get out of the way," said the butcher, " or I'll slam this *ship* in your face." At this moment Smollett's foot slipped, and catching hold of the butcher's arm to save his fall, both fell in the gutter, which was streaming with blood from the slaughter-houses. The butcher recovered himself first, and in rising gave Smollett a violent blow in the face with his bloody fist. Poor Smollett scrambled up as well as he could, all covered with gore ; got into a shop, and there remained till a coach was procured to carry him home. He then resided in a court leading out of Dean-street, Soho. When he arrived, the children of the neighbourhood, seeing a man streaked with blood get out

* See D'Israeli's Calamities of Authors, vol. ii. 2. " Akenside's mind and manners," says the author, " were of a fine, romantic cast."

of the coach, surrounded the house, and the whole place was kept for some time in a state of suspense and confusion. A constable was sent for to search the house, where *the bloody man* had been taken; and it was a long time before the crowd could be pacified and dispersed. Smollett lodged there only a few weeks after; during which time he was frequently hailed by the children, " *There goes the bloody man.*"

Hearing that an opening for a physician presented itself at Northampton, Akenside went thither with an intention of establishing himself. But Dr. Stonehouse being in full practice, as he found soon after his arrival, and not relishing, as the vulgar saying is, the art of waiting for dead men's shoes, he returned to London after a stay of about a year and a half; and the only interesting circumstance, connected with his residence there, is an account, furnished us by Dr. Kippis; who says, that when he resided at Northampton, he well remembered hearing Dr. Doddridge and Dr. Akenside carry on an amicable debate " concerning the opinions of the ancient philosophers, with regard to a future state of rewards and punishments; in which Akenside supported the firm belief of Cicero in particular, in this great article of natural religion."

This argument calls to our recollection an assertion of Dr. Doddridge on another occasion, that "men of contrary parties sit down more attached to their own opinions than they were at the beginning, and much more estranged in affection."

As we have no data, on which to build any opinion as to the precise time, in which several of Akenside's odes were written, we are left to our own conjectures; and as Akenside had much leisure during his stay at Northampton, we may naturally suppose that he engaged no small portion of that leisure in literary occupation. To this leisure, perhaps, therefore, we may be indebted for his ode on " Lyric Poetry ;" for that on " the Uses of Poetry ;" and for that to " the Muse."

The first of these odes has always been classed with the sublime. The characters of Anacreon, Alcæus, and Pindar, are finely drawn ; but that of Sappho is injudicious ; and the more so, since the prophecy was not fulfilled.

> " Why is my faithful maid distrest?
> Who, Sappho, wounds thy tender breast ?
> Say, flies he ? soon he shall pursue:
> Shews he thy gifts ? He soon shall give :
> Slights he thy sorrows ? He shall grieve,
> And soon to all thy wishes bow."
>
> *St.* ii. 1.

The simile,

> "As eagles drink the noontide flame,"
>
> *St.* ii. 2.

is far-fetched ; and the idea in a preceding stanza is in a manner not superior to that of Waller:

> " His cheek displays a second spring
> Of roses, taught by wine to bloom."
>
> *St.* i. 2.

But his allusions to himself are always in the best style of egotism. That in the last stanza is little inferior to any similar instance in Cassimir or Buchanan.

In respect to the ode " on the Influence of Poetry," Akenside seems to have been, at all times, deeply impressed with the important influence of that powerful art on the manners, happiness, and opinions of mankind. This is amply testified in this ode, as well as in that to his Muse ; and still more strictly inculcated in the episode of Solon, in the third book of his second poem on the Imagination, which seems to have been expressly written to prove the same result.

Finding Northampton not to afford any advantageous opportunity for the exercise of his medical talents, Akenside returned to London ; and soon after Mr. Dyson bought a house at North-end, Hampstead; and with a view of introducing his friend to the more opulent inhabitants, he frequented with him the long room, and all the clubs and assemblies. He, also, had the extraordinary generosity to allow him three hundred pounds a year, till he should be able to live by his practice, like a gentleman.

And now we have leisure to make a few remarks on Akenside's sensibility to the softer sex. He never married; but in the ode he wrote about this time, viz. that to SIR FRANCIS HENRY DRAKE, BART.—there is a stanza, remarkable for its allusion to a lady, whom he styles OLYMPIA :—

" ———— Thy stubborn breast,
Though touch'd by many a slighter wound,
Hath no full conquest yet confest,
Nor the one fatal charmer found.
While I, a true and loyal swain,
My fair OLYMPIA's gentle reign
Through all the varying seasons own ;
Her genius still my bosom warms,
No other maid for me hath charms ;
And I have eyes for her alone."

St. viii.

Previous to this, however, the poet seems to have entertained an affection for a young lady, whom he alludes to in the second book of the Pleasures of Imagination, under the name of PARTHENIA; and who seems to have died at a time when he was about to be married to her. At least, such must be our impression on reading the following passage:

—————————— " Of good and evil much,
And much of mortal man, my thought revolv'd ;
When starting full on fancy's gushing eye,
The mournful image of PARTHENIA's fate,—
(That hour, O long beloved and long deplor'd !)|
When blooming youth, nor gentlest wisdom's arts,
Nor Hymen's honours gather'd for thy brow,
Nor all the lover's, all the father's tears,
Avail'd, to snatch thee from the cruel grave,—
Thy agonizing looks, thy last farewell,
Struck to the inmost feeling of my soul,
As with the hand of death !"

P. I. B. ii. 191.

Who Parthenia was, and who Olympia, it is now useless to inquire. He nowhere mentions their real names, and his biographers have not only neglected to inquire, but even to be unconscious, that such persons ever existed.

His love for Olympia, at the time he resided at Hampstead, seems to have been in an early stage ; little, if any thing, more than friendship : but in a subsequent ode he lets us into the secret,

that friendship is but too often another name for
love :

> " Once I remember, new to love,
>   And dreading his tyrannic chain,
>   I sought a gentle maid to prove
>   What peaceful joys in friendship reign,
>   Whence we, forsooth, might safely stand,
>   And pitying view the lovesick band,
> And mock the winged boy's malicious hand.
>
>   Thus frequent pass'd the cloudless day,
>   To smiles and sweet discourse resign'd ;
>   While I exulted to survey
>   One generous woman's real mind ;
>   Till friendship soon my languid breast
>   Each night with unknown cares possest,
> Dash'd my coy slumbers, or my dreams distrest.
>
>   Fool that I was !—and now, e'en now,
>   While thus I preach the stoic strain,
>   Unless I shun Olympia's view,
>   An hour unsays it all again.
>   O friend !—when love directs her eyes,
>   To pierce where every passion lies,
> Where is the firm, the cautious, or the wise?"

The poet seems to have forgotten the manner in
which he had ridiculed the lover in former times * ;
as well as the tone, he had assumed, in his Ode to a
friend, unsuccessful in love †.

* See P. I., B. iii. 170.
† This friend was Mr. EDWARDS, whom we shall have

In his Elegy on Love we are let a little more into the real state of things:

" Too much my heart of beauty's power has known,
Too long to love hath reason left her throne;
Too long my genius mourn'd his myrtle chain,
And three rich years of youth consum'd in vain."

To this subject we shall return at a future opportunity. At present we must turn to a less pleasing one; that of a friend of Akenside having taken a causeless jealousy against his wife, for some innocent freedoms, in which she had indulged; such as walking, one evening, home from a party

occasion, hereafter, to mention in a more particular manner. The state of his mind may be easily conjectured from a sonnet, he addressed to Mr. Wray, on this unfortunate occasion.

" Trust me, dear Wray, not all these three months' pain,
Though tedious seems the time in pain to wear;
Nor all those restless nights, through which in vain
I've sought for kindly sleep to lull my care;
Nor all those lonely meals, and meagre fare,
Uncheer'd with converse, and a friendly guest,
This close confinement, barr'd from wholesome air,
And exercise, of medicines the best,
Have sunk my spirits, or my soul oppress'd.
Light are *these* woes, and easy to be borne;
If weigh'd with those, which rack'd my tortur'd breast,
When my fond heart from AMORET was torn:
So true the word of Solomon to find,
' No shaft so piercing as the wounded mind.'"

E

with a gentleman, who offered to escort her, and whom she had known almost from infancy. His name was THURLOE. Akenside's friend was a gentleman, with whom he had become acquainted at Edinburgh; but whose name I do not remember.

This friend, in his distress, did not fail to apply to Akenside for advice; and the poet, learning how little he had to build his suspicions upon, remonstrated with him strongly on the cruelty of subjecting his family to the consequences of so odious an imputation; and, as a still farther caution, wrote him an ode against the dangers of suspicion. The first five stanzas of this ode are very powerful; and remind us, strongly, of several passages in Othello.

> " Oh fly! It's dire Suspicion's mien,
> And, meditating plagues unseen,
>   The Sorceress hither bends;
> Behold her torch in gall imbru'd;
> Behold—her garment drops with blood
>   Of lovers and of friends.
>
> Fly far! already in your eyes
> I see a pale suffusion rise;
>   And soon through every vein,
> Soon will her secret venom spread,
> And all your heart, and all your head,
>   Imbibe the potent stain.

Then many a demon will she raise,
To vex your sleep, to haunt your ways;
   While gleams of lost delight
Raise the dark tempest of the brain,
As lightning shines across the main
   Through whirlwinds and through night.

No more can faith or candour move;
But each ingenuous deed of love,
   Which reason would applaud,
Now smiling o'er her dark distress,
Fancy, malignant, strives to dress
   Like injury and fraud.

Farewell to virtue's peaceful times;
Soon will you stoop to act the crimes,
   Which thus you stoop to fear.
Guilt follows guilt; and where the train
Begins with wrongs of such a stain,
   What horrors form the rear!"

The closing stanzas are very beautiful :

" O thou! whate'er thy awful name,
   Whose wisdom our untoward frame
     With social love restrains;
   Thou! who, by fair affection's ties,
   Giv'st us to double all our joys,
     And half disarm our pains;

   Let universal candour still,
   Clear as yon heaven-reflecting rill,
     Preserve my open mind;

E 2

> Nor this, nor that man's crooked ways
> One sordid doubt within me raise;
> To injure human kind *."

In 1746, Akenside wrote his ode to *the Evening Star*; an ode, which, though it recalls to our memory Collins' Ode to Evening, can never be read without pleasure; particularly the following stanza:

> " Oh ! think o'er all this mortal stage,
> What mournful scenes arise ;
> What ruin waits on kingly rage ;
> How often virtue dwells with woe ;
> How many griefs from knowledge flow ;
> How swiftly pleasure flies."

This stanza calls to our recollection a still more beautiful one in Gray's poem on the Pleasures arising from Vicissitude.

> " Still where rosy pleasure leads,
> See a kindred grief pursue ;
> Behind the steps that misery treads,
> Approaching comfort view :

---

* Mr. Alison quotes three stanzas from this ode (vi. vii. viii.) " in which," says he, " a scene, which is, in general, only beautiful, is rendered strikingly sublime, from the imagery with which it is connected."—*Of the Nature of the Emotions of Beauty and Sublimity*, p. 19, 20, 21.

The hues of bliss more brightly glow,
Chastised to sober tints of woe:
And, blended, form, with artful strife,
The strength and harmony of life."

In this year Akenside sent a paper, which he had written in imitation of the 81st number of the Tatler, and which he entitled the TABLE OF MODERN FAME, to Dodsley for insertion in a periodical work, he was then publishing, entitled the MUSEUM, It is a curious and interesting paper; and I ascribe it to Akenside on the authority of WARTON, who, in a note to a passage in Pope *, characterizes it as a paper of great taste and judgment.

THE TABLE OF MODERN FAME.

A VISION.

" LAST night, after leaving the company, where I had spent the evening, I took up a volume of the Tatler, to conclude the day. I happened to light on that admired paper †, where the most celebrated personages of antiquity are represented at the table of Fame. I was very agreeably amused with the venerable assembly, and the pleasing manner in which they are introduced; till I had

---

* See his Edition of Pope, vol. ii. 83.
† No. 81.

formed my own mind to that composure and stillness,
which is the best preparative to a happy repose.

" As soon as I fell asleep, methought I was walking
in an immense plain, where I met a figure of great dignity, representing a man in the full vigour of his age,
clothed in a purple garment, with a rod of silver in his
hand.   He accosted me: and I learned from his discourse, that he had formerly lived upon our earth ; but
that now he was raised to the enjoyment of that felicity,
which God had appointed for the reward of prudence
and virtue.   ' I see,' said he, ' young man, that you
are just returned from the mansion of *Ancient Fame ;*
and I perceive by your countenance that you have not
been thoroughly satisfied with the goddess of the place,
or with the order of that assembly, over which she pre-
sides.   You mortals are prone to imagine, that the
smiles of *Fame* are always bestowed according to the
suffrage of Virtue ; but in this you find you are mistaken.
If your curiosity incline you to inquire into the management of *Modern Fame,* the younger sister, follow me,
and I will conduct you to her abode.'

" Immediately he led me to a very spacious building, of a mixed and crude sort of architecture, where,
though I admired the expensiveness of the materials,
yet the ornaments, methought, were ill designed, and
of a vulgar taste; like a clumsy ungraceful person,
dressed out in jewels and embroidery.   I was particularly disgusted to see among the ancient festoons of
flowers, pipes, and musical reeds, which were adjusted
to the columns of the temple, mitres, and triple crowns,
crosiers, and other ensigns of ecclesiastical discipline.

This building was surrounded with an innumerable crowd of people; and at each of the spacious doors, which opened on every side of it, I observed a tall, majestical woman, attended with a crowd of figures, some like men with large volumes in their hands, and others resembling the descriptions which poets have given us of the MUSES. These women, as my conductor informed me, were the guardians or genii of the several nations of the world. The historians and the Muses were for ever moving from one to another, yet, I observed, that they never visited some of the gates, where the women were almost naked, or dressed in turbans and painted feathers.

" We entered the temple :—at the upper end sate the goddess, on a throne of a very uncommon structure. It was composed of different materials, laid up in a beautiful architonick manner. I observed, that military instruments, as standards, swords, and pieces of artillery, most frequently appeared in the architecture; yet I likewise cast my eye on telescopes, rudders, painting pallets, geometrical schemes, and instruments of handicraft. By the looks and motions of people within the temple, I guessed that we were come just in time to be present at some great ceremony; for I observed the Muses and historians stepping ever and anon from some or other of the gates, and whispering the goddess, who gave each of them directions, which I could not hear. I asked my conductor the purpose of this great preparation; and what meant the twenty thrones which I counted round the temple, and why some of them were quite empty, while others were laid hold of by certain persons, who stood behind them, as if they were waiting for leave to sit down.

" He answered me in the following manner : ' You are come from the table of *Ancient Fame*. The goddess there disposed of her honours without reserve or conditional change : her youngest sister is not so constant. Once in every century she reviews her assembly, and frequently makes great alterations, removing her subjects from one seat to a lower, or a higher ; admitting strangers, or entirely excluding her former favourites. To-day is the anniversary of her great establishment : the empty seats formerly belonged to those whom she has now entirely banished from her palace. Those persons, whom you see standing behind some of the thrones, have leave to renew their claim ; and if no other candidates obtain their place, will continue in the order which formerly belonged to them.'

" While he was speaking, the goddess rose from her seat, and commanded the several nations in her presence to introduce their candidates in the order which she had enjoined them. Upon this all the crowd of spectators disappeared, and the temple was left quite empty. After a short pause, the trumpet of the goddess sounded ; the whole fabric shook ; and my heart was filled with a rapture and astonishment which I never felt before.

"Immediately the temple was crowded again, and from the uppermost gate entered the most beautiful of those divine women, the GENIUS of ITALY. She led in a middle-aged man, in a very plain dress, who held in his hand a mariner's compass. The spectators, whose coun-

tenances expressed the most impatient suspense, gave a
confused acclamation, and I heard at once from a hundred mouths the name of COLUMBUS. He advanced
towards the goddess, and sat down on the highest place,
with an air of ease ; as if that seat had long been familiar to him. ' That,' said my conductor, ' is the man
who has enabled history to outdo fable : nor are the
actions of the *Grecian Hercules,* either for greatness of
imagination, or for boldness, or utility, comparable to
the discovery of the new world ; yet, perhaps, you will,
this day, see another take place of him.'

" The trumpet sounded a second time :—while I was
expecting some other personage from the gates nearest
to the goddess, I observed a great hurry at the very
lowest end of the temple. A woman, whom I had
before taken notice of among those, who appeared almost
naked and wild, advanced from her gate in a robe of
furs, and other skins, and approached towards the goddess. The genii at the upper end expressed a mixture
of surprise and indignation, that so savage a figure
should now dare to step before them. As she drew
near, I observed the person whom she conducted ; he
was a robust man in armour, with his own hair, a black
eagle on his breast, and a carpenter's axe in his hand.
I knew his habit, and with the crowd pronounced hastily
the name of PETER the GREAT. He sat down on the
second throne, and I could not help applauding the
justice of the goddess.

" The third person who appeared was conducted by
the representative of Italy, but the moment he set his

foot within the temple, the Muses and all the attendant
powers from the other gates ran up at once to usher
him. He seemed between thirty and forty years of age.
The lyric, the comic, and the heroic muse, a winged
virgin with a lyre, another with a pallet, a third with a
chisel and block of marble, and an infinite number of
beautiful young figures, did him honour as he passed.
He returned their congratulations with smiles of the
highest complacence, and seemed pleased with his introduction, chiefly as it secured him such amiable companions. By his pontifical robes I knew him for LEO X.

"But our next personage was ushered in a very different manner. He entered from the German gate; a
great noise of disputants and logical terms preceded him;
his face had a very bold, eager cast; his eyes were
keen, and his dress monkish. When he came to sit
down, seeing Leo on the throne next above him, he fell
into a violent rage, and would needs have rose again.
Leo, on the other hand, turned from him with a smile
of high contempt, and begged of the beautiful powers,
who stood around him, that they would 'hide that rude
creature from his eyes, and defend his ears with their
harmony, from the jargon which he uttered.'

" I was vexed at his being thrust into so unsuitable a
neighbourhood, and asked my guide, who he was? 'His
name,' said he, 'is MARTIN LUTHER. He has done
more good to mankind, than most of those, whose inten-
tions were the best and most heroic; his character, his
views, and passions, were contemptible and hateful.
Remember what I told you—' Fame does not proceed

on the award of wisdom or virtue; but is governed solely by the revolutions of mortal things*.''

" I was angry and disappointed, that I had yet seen none of my countrymen, when the trumpet sounded, and I beheld a figure entering from one of the upper gates, with a red cross upon her shield, leading a venerable man in the decline of life. I remembered the face of Sir Isaac Newton. He advanced in a very composed manner, without speaking a word, or seeming to take notice of the acclamations, which came from every part of the temple.

" All eyes were fixed upon him, and all were proud, that they had seen him: yet I observed a man at the *French* gate, dressed in a very gaudy, fantastic habit, who repined bitterly, that his place was taken from him; while the guardian deity of its nation seemed to be musing upon a thousand schemes how to regain it,

---

* " Fame is not determined, nor is it ever determinable, by a right judgment of men and things. A conqueror of kingdoms, who puts thousands to death, and reduces ten times their number to poverty and want, rises so high in fame, that the remotest posterity never mention his name, but with admiration and rapture. The generality of the world cannot distinguish accurately between splendour and greatness; and, therefore, the *plurality* of the *voices* would, doubtless, be in favour of military heroes."—*Tatler, No.* 81. *note.*

" The opinions, declared in this paper, are not opinions of characters, but opinions of reputations; the decisions are not with regard to merit, but with regard to fame, and the refusal of the one is no denial of the other."—*Ibid.*

There was a man, too, who advanced impudently from
the *German* gate; and would have driven Newton, by
force, from his seat.   He was a very odd figure, with a
nightcap on his head, a mathematical diagram in one
hand, and a bottle of Rhenish in the other.   The goddess
ordered him to be chastised for a robber, and turned out
with infamy.

" At the next trumpet, the gay lady, whose robes
were flowered with lilies, left her favourite, DESCARTES,
about whom, till that moment, she had been so solicitous,
and turned to introduce a tall, graceful man, who
walked along in a full-bottomed wig, with infinite self-
applause.   When he saw Leo, he made a very com-
plaisant bow; yet, as Shakspeare says, *he quenched
his familiar smile, with an austere regard of control.*
I suppose it was LOUIS THE FOURTEENTH, and com-
plained to my guide, that such a man should be so
honoured.   ' Have patience,' said he; ' meet me here
a hundred years hence, and you shall see the goddess
order him underground, to the house of *Evil Fame.* At
present she must have her way.   Look round, and see
if you are better satisfied with him, who comes next.'
I saw a composed matron-like figure bring in a man in
armour, with signs of the highest veneration and gratitude.   ' That,' said my conductor, ' is WILLIAM I.,
PRINCE OF ORANGE ; a name, that must be venerable
upon your globe, as long as public virtue is remembered
among you; and of this divine man, I can prophesy,
that he will never lose his place.   The youth, who is
now entering, will, perhaps, give you more pleasure ;
and indeed though his merits and actions are not of so

high a kind, yet his virtue shone, perhaps, in a more severe trial, in a course of uninterrupted prosperity; so that if his times had given him an opportunity, he was equal to any thing, which can be acted by a man and a soldier.'

" I looked around, and beheld, from the English gate, a young man in armour, with a spear of ebony, and beautiful as Raphael or Milton could imagine. ' You need not,' said I, ' tell me who this is: I see the motto of *Wales* on his shield, and the sable spear in his hand, which has rendered the name of EDWARD, or of PLANTAGENET, useless. All hail! thou blameless ornament of my native country————.' I was going on in a kind of enthusiasm, when my conductor checked me, and bade me take notice of the next, who entered. I found a greater noise and disorder, than I had observed before. *Germany* and *Spain* had joined to introduce a coarse, robust man; and *France* endeavoured to place before him a tall, majestic person, with a crown on his head, who looked upon his antagonist with an air of reproach and disdain. This was FRANCIS I. However, his opponent got the better, and took his place accordingly. By the imperial eagle, which he wore on his breast, I supposed it to be CHARLES V. At sitting down, he laughed at his adversary—' and,' says he, ' if I must have given way, it should never have been to that doubty, romantic knight, my prisoner; but to this great man, who gave me immortality,' pointing to Titian, who stood in the crowd of his attendants.

" The next person, that entered, was dressed in a morning gown, and ushered in by the Lady of the Red

Cross. He had no symbol nor instrument in his hand; but shewed a very thoughtful and penetrating countenance. He walked up in profound silence, and made no return, but a look of grave displeasure, to the salutation of his next neighbour. However, he took very respectful notice of some at the table; particularly of *Columbus* and *Newton*. *Leo* seemed afraid of him; *Luther* made him a very gracious bow, and would have been extremely intimate with him; but received a cold and forbidding frown. By this account of him, the reader will know as well as I did, who saw what passed, that this was LOCKE. The next entrance was made from the *Italian* gate, and there appeared a thin, meagre man, whose countenance expressed great pain and dejection of spirit, as if he had been worn out by famine and torture. He held in his hand a telescope; and my conductor told me it was GALILEO, whose face retained indelible marks of the blind, brutal, zeal of his ghostly tormentors.

" He sat down by *Locke*, who seemed infinitely pleased with his company; and told him that he had been endeavouring to cure mankind of that stupid reverence for ruffians and murderers, who masked their inhumanity with the name of religion.

" After the next trumpet there was a long pause, and nobody appeared. I heard a great bustle at the *German* gate. The goddess asked what was the matter. The robust *German* tutelary made answer, that she was introducing one, who, if useful discoveries could challenge respect in that place, was, perhaps, entitled to the highest seat. Immediately I heard words of a very

rough sound.   *Guttenberg, Fust, Mentz, Strasburgh!*
I then understood that the crowd of Germans, at that
gate, were disputing which of them should enter as the
discoverer of printing.   The contest continued a long
time, and grew still more violent, upon which the
goddess spoke out, that when they could agree about
the inventor, she would frankly allow his claim; but
that, till then, she would put in his place one, whose
merit and whose glory was now unquestionably established, after as great disputes about it, as had ever
divided her subjects.

   " Upon this she made a sign to the red-cross lady,
who accordingly introduced a venerable old man, whom
I did not at all know.   He was attended by a female
figure with a patera in her hand, resembling the ancient
figures of *Salus*.   I was surprised at the sight of an
English worthy, with whom I was not acquainted; but
my guide informed me, that his name was HARVEY;
' and see,' says he, ' how enviously those other tutelar
genii regard him;' pointing to *France* and *Italy*.

   " The trumpet again sounded, and the guardian of
Italy moved.   As soon as she returned, there was a confused noise of *Evil Fame!* and *downward with him!* a
great herd of priests and monks, and prime ministers,
joined in the cry; and amongst them there was a young
man, with a crown on his head, who made the loudest
noise, and who assured the goddess of Fame, that the
person coming in was an abandoned profligate, and that
he himself had a much better title to the next vacant
seat.

   " The goddess looked on him with great contempt,

and bid him hold his peace, else she would order him below stairs, and put him again under his father's tuition. At this he was silent, and MACHIAVEL appeared. Leo gave him a very familiar look, as if he was glad to see him, and congratulated him upon the honour, which he had now obtained, of being seated at the same table with one of the great family, who had been his old patrons. But Machiavel answered him only with a look of shame, dislike, and indignation. The Italian genius moved again towards the gate, and returned with two men, not being able to resolve which of them should enter. These were TASSO and ARIOSTO. She herself inclined chiefly to the latter; but the majority of the spectators opposed it, and TASSO took his place.

" At the next trumpet the tutelary of *France* went out with the assured air, that was natural to her, and brought in a tall, slender man, in a large wig, with a very fine sneer upon his face. She said his name was BOILEAU; and that nobody could pretend to dispute that place with him. However, the stately genius of *England* opposed her. Her remonstrances prevailed, and POPE took the place, which Boileau thought belonged to him. Upon this there arose among the other genii a great clamour against the *red-cross lady*, mixed with many signs of ridicule and scorn. She asked what they were displeased at, that she should contend so eagerly for her own glory, and yet so obstinately reject a claim, upon which she might best found it; and which, whenever she advanced it, they would all give way to. She turned round, and saw BACON ready to enter, without asking her to conduct him. She looked at him with great disgust; yet with such an air as a tender mother discovers, when her favourite child is guilty of some inexcusable fault. She led him in with great reluctance, and shewed him his place, the next vacant one below Pope. He stood, and looked upon it; and all the spectators seemed ashamed that he had not a higher seat. Locke, Newton, Harvey, and Machiavel, all cried out to Pope, ' Do rise, and give place:' but he took no notice of them, only he turned his head another way; and I heard him mutter the words, ' *wisest, brightest, meanest.*' Upon this Bacon looked around, and drew the eyes of all the assembly. His presence, at that time, had an effect upon them, like the presence of a descended god upon those mortals, whom he favours with his converse. Then raising his head, ' Sure I am,' said he, ' that if there be any place belonging to me in this assembly, it must be one, nearest to the goddess; and one, where I may best avail myself of her power.'

" Immediately the assembly, with one accord, invited him forward; the goddess beckoning him to draw near; and seated him on the highest throne. Columbus himself officiously gave way; telling him ' that the discovery of a new world was but a slender acquisition of crude materials, to be improved and perfected in that immense world of human knowledge and human power, which he had first discovered, and through which he had taught other mortals to travel with security.'

" The next that entered, was a man in iron armour, with a basket-hilted sword. *France, Germany,* and *Italy* turned pale at the sight of him; and I heard them whisper the name of GUSTAVUS ADOLPHUS. He

F

was followed by a beautiful youth, of a very sweet and gentle aspect. As he drew nearer, I knew him to be RAPHAEL. Leo heard of his admission with an extravagant joy, and could hardly be restrained from quitting his place, that he might sit next him. Then appeared a blind, old man, with the air of an ancient prophet, supported and led in by the genius of England. When I knew him I was extremely discontented, that no more honourable place had been reserved for MILTON. ‘ You forget,’ said my conductor, ‘ that the lowest place in this assembly, is one of twenty, the most honourable gifts, which Fame has to bestow among the whole human species. Milton is now admitted for the first time, and was not, but with difficulty admitted at all. But have patience for a few years longer: he will be continually ascending in the goddess's favour, and may, perhaps, at last, obtain the highest, or at least the second place in these her solemnities. In the mean time see how he is received by the man, who is best qualified here to judge of his dignity.'

“ I looked at him again, and saw Raphael making him the most affectionate congratulations, accounting himself happy, that he was seated next to him, and insisting on his taking the superior hand.

“ There now remained but one place to be disposed of. The tutelar deity of *Spain* led in, towards it, a slender man, with black piercing eyes, an aquiline nose, and a swarthy complexion. He had lost one of his hands, by which mark I knew him to be CERVANTES. He expected no opposition, as the place had formerly belonged to him ; but in this point he was mistaken.

For Moliere advanced from the *French* entrance, and disputed the chair, with infinite pleasantry and good-humour. Cervantes, however, kept his place ; but while their controversy was hardly yet decided, a third candidate appeared, with a great shout of clamorous mirth from the whole assembly. They told me, he had brushed in by stealth, and in spite of the grave lady, who conducted his countrymen. I knew the arch leer, the nut-brown bays, and the Foppington step of my facetious friend, Colley Cibber. But his appearance, his arguments, and the eloquence with which he delivered them, quite disjointed the remainder of my dream, and I waked in a very hearty fit of laughter *."

It is very remarkable, that in this vision the author should have omitted the greatest of his countrymen, SHAKESPEARE ; and the more so, since, from several passages in his works, we are left in no doubt as to the manner, in which he appreciated that wonderful poet.

The year 1746 was rendered, also, interesting to Akenside by his having produced his HYMN TO THE NAIADS. Johnson superciliously passes over, as unworthy of being read, not only Akenside's odes, but even this truly elegant hymn—a hymn so entirely classical, that we have not one more

* Museum, No. xiii. Sept. 13, 1746.

so in our language; hence Lloyd, with great propriety, in allusion to Homer's hymns, which he
had once an intention of translating, says—" They,
who would form the justest idea of this sort of
composition among the ancients, may be better informed, by perusing Dr. Akenside's most classical
Hymn to the Naiads, than from any translation of
Homer or Callimachus."

The beauties of this hymn, the title of which,
perhaps, gave birth to Dr. Southey's beautiful
HYMN TO THE PENATES, are too numerous and
too well known to warrant quotation.   The passage
beginning with

> ————" Haunt beloved of sylvan powers,
> Of nymphs and fauns," &c. &c.

seems to be derived from a passage in Lucretius:

> " Hæc loca capripedes Satyros, nymphasque, tenere
> Finitumei fingunt: et Faunos esse loquuntur,
> Quorum," &c.
>
> De Rerum Natura, iv. 584.

Or, perhaps, more immediately from Martial:

> " Sæpe sub hoc madidi luserunt arbore Fauni
> Terruit et tacitam fistula sera domum;
> Dumque fugit solos nocturnum Pana per agros,
> Sæpe sub hac latuit rustica fronde Dryas."
>
> Ep. lib. ix. 62. xii. 11.

The lines, beginning with

——————— " Those powerful strings,
That charm the mind of gods," &c.

illustrative of the effects of sacred music among the
gods, is taken from the first Pythian ode of Pindar.
The translation is very beautiful.

The notes to this poem indicate a considerable
share of learning; and are, no doubt, helps to the
unlettered; but to the learned, I should suppose,
they must operate as incumbrances. That, however, in which the poet gives an account of what he
intended, in the construction of his hymn *, is very

* " Cyrene was the native country of Callimachus, whose
hymns are the most remarkable example of that mythological
passion, which is assumed in the preceding poem, and have
always afforded particular pleasure to the author of it, by
reason of the mysterious solemnity with which they affect
the mind. On this account he was induced to attempt
somewhat in the same manner, solely by way of exercise;
the manner itself being now almost entirely abandoned in
poetry: and as the mere genealogy, or the personal adven-
ture, of heathen gods could have been but little interesting
to a modern reader, it was, therefore, thought proper to
select some convenient part of the history of nature: and to
employ these ancient divinities, as it is probable, they were
first employed, to wit, in personifying natural causes, and in
representing the mutual agreement or opposition of the cor-
poreal and moral powers of the world, which hath been
accounted the very highest office of poetry."

important; and ought continually to be borne in mind by the critic, as well as by the general reader.

Hampstead could not be suited to a man like Akenside. The inhabitants were respectable and rich; but many of them were not only respectable and rich, but purse-proud, and, therefore, supercilious. They required to be sought; their wives and daughters expected to be escorted and flattered; and their sons to be treated with an air of obligation. It is no difficult task for an elegant man to flatter beautiful women and celebrated men; but to be subservient to those, who are already too vain and supercilious, and who assume in proportion as they are flattered and yielded to, is not only beyond the practice, but even beyond the honest patience, of a man enriched by nature and embellished by education *. After residing two

* This observation naturally reminds me of the fate of Dr. Sewell, author of a tragedy, entitled *Sir Walter Raleigh*, who died at Hampstead in 1726; and whose melancholy fate is thus related by Mr. Campbell, author of the Pleasures of Hope: —

" He was a physician at Hampstead, with very little practice, and chiefly subsisted on the invitations of the neighbouring gentlemen, to whom his amiable character made him acceptable; but at his death not a friend or relative came to commit his remains to the dust. He was buried in the meanest manner, under a hollow tree, that was once part of

years and a half at Hampstead, therefore, Akenside returned to London, and took up his abode in Bloomsbury-square, where he continued to live during the remainder of his life. He was now about seven and twenty.

" In London," says one of his biographers, " Akenside was well-known as a poet ;—but he had still to make himself known as a physician :"—and he would have been put to great straits, had not the generous friendship of Mr. Dyson enabled him to preserve the appearance of a gentleman. These two friends seem to have acted strictly in the character of ancient times ; so well delineated by those writers, to whose works they were so peculiarly devoted, viz. Plato, Cicero, Plutarch, Marcus Antoninus, and Epictetus (in Arrian).

Akenside's friend took every opportunity of introducing him ; and being a man of fortune and high respectability, the natural consequence was a due appreciation of Akenside's merit,—as a physician and a man of elegance,—by many persons of superior station.

In 1747, having heard a sermon preached, in

the boundary of the churchyard of Hampstead. No memorial was placed over his remains."—*Specimens of the Poets,* v. i.

which the reverend divine declaimed, in a very urgent manner, against Glory, he wrote an ode in opposition to the exhortations of the preacher. Part of this ode must be again quoted ; not only because it instructs us, as to the poet's opinions on that sub‑ject, but because it will serve as a proper introduc‑tion to another subject, which seems once to have engaged some portion of his ambition.

> " Come, then, tell me, sage divine !
>   Is it an offence to own
> That our bosoms e'er incline
>   Toward immortal glory's throne ?
> For with me, nor pomp, nor pleasure,
> Bourbon's might, Braganza's treasure,
> So can Fancy's dream rejoice,
> So conciliate Reason's choice,
> As one approving word of her impartial voice.
>
> If to spurn at noble praise
>   Be the passport to thy heav'n,
> Follow thou these gloomy ways :
>   No such law to me was given.
> Nor, I trust, shall I deplore me :
> Faring like my friends before me,
> Nor an holier place desire,
> Than TIMOLEON's arms acquire,
> And Tully's curule chair, and Milton's golden lyre."

TIMOLEON seems to have been, of all others in ancient times, the hero, that most engaged Aken‑

side's admiration ; and he extended that admiration even so far, as to have meditated the writing an epic poem, of which that illustrious patriot should be the hero. This project he alludes to in the last stanza of his ode on Lyric Poetry.

> " But when from envy and from death to claim
>   A hero bleeding for his native land,
> When to throw incense on the vestal's flame
>   Of liberty my genius gives command,
> Nor Theban voice, nor Lesbian lyre
> From thee, O muse ! do I require,
>   While my presaging mind,
> Conscious of powers she never knew,
> Astonish'd grasps at things beyond her view,
> Nor by *another's fate* submits to be confined."

Akenside told Warton *, that he alluded, in the last line, to the LEONIDAS OF GLOVER, which he looked upon as a failure.

Pope had once the same design ; and the same subject had also been proposed by Lord Melcombe to the author of the Seasons. Why Pope dropped his intention does not appear ; the reasons of Thomson are thus stated in a letter to Lord Melcombe †. " If any thing could make me capable of an epic performance, it would be your favourable opinion in thinking so. But (as you justly observe) that must

* Warton's Pope, ii. 73. *Ed.* 1797.   † Oct. 24, 1730.

be the work of years, and one must be in an epic situation to execute it. My heart both trembles with diffidence and burns with ardour at the thought. The story of TIMOLEON is good as to the subject matter: but an author owes, I think, the scene of an epic action to his own country; besides, Timoleon admits of no machinery; except that of the heathen gods, which will not do at this time of day. I hope hereafter to have the direction of your taste in these affairs; and in the meantime will endeavour to expand those ideas and sentiments, and in some degree to gather up that knowledge, which is necessary to such an undertaking."

Why Akenside did not prosecute the design he meditated, we have now no means of ascertaining. Perhaps, he considered the difficulty of the subject; or he might feel some reluctance to engage further in pursuits, that might obstruct the practice he was solicitous, at this time, to obtain. This, I think, may be inferred from a passage in his Ode to Sleep.

> " Oh let me not alone complain,
>   Alone invoke thy power in vain !
>   Descend, propitious, on my eyes ;
>   Not from the couch, that bears a crown,
>   Not from the courtly statesman's down,
>   Nor where the miser and his treasure lies:

Bring not the shapes, that break the murderer's rest,
  Nor those, the bireling soldier loves to see,
Nor those which haunt the bigot's gloomy breast;
  Far be their guilty nights, and far their dreams from me.

  Nor yet their awful forms present,
  For chiefs and heroes only meant;
    The figured brass, the choral song,
  The rescued people's glad applause,
  The listening senate, and the laws,
    Fix'd by the counsels of Timoleon's tongue,
Are scenes too grand for Fortune's private ways;
And though they shine in youth's ingenuous view,
The sober, gainful, arts of modern days
  To such romantic thoughts have bid a long adieu."

Akenside had been admitted, by mandamus, to a doctor's degree at Cambridge; he became a fellow of the Royal Society; and was elected a fellow of the Royal College of Physicians. Mr. Dyson, on the other hand, had entered himself at one of the Inns of Court, and been called to the bar. But in the early part of this year (1747), hearing that Mr. Hardinge had the intention of retiring from the clerkship of the House of Commons, he entered into a treaty with that gentleman, and purchased the situation for six thousand pounds. And here I cannot deny myself the pleasure of citing a very striking characteristic of Mr. Dyson, from Hatsell's

Precedents of the Proceedings of the House of Commons.

On the 15th of February Mr. Dyson took his seat at the table *. " By virtue of his office," says Mr. Hatsell, " the clerk has not only the right of appointing a deputy to officiate in his stead, but has the nomination of the clerk assistant, and all the other clerks without doors. Formerly the appointment to these offices made a considerable part of the clerk's income, as it was the usual practice to sell them. But when Mr. Dyson came to the office of clerk, (though he had purchased this of Mr. Hardinge for no less a sum than six thousand pounds,) he, with a generosity peculiar to himself, and from a regard to the House of Commons, that the several under-clerkships might be more properly filled, than they probably would be, if they were sold to the highest bidder, first refused this

* " On the 10th of February, 1747, the Speaker acquaints the House of Commons with a letter he had received from Nicholas Hardinge, Esq. clerk, in which he informs him, that he had resigned the office ;—Mr. Speaker also acquaints the House, that his Majesty will in a few days appoint another person to succeed Mr. Hardinge ; and on the 15th of February, Mr. Dyson being appointed, is called in, and takes his seat at the table."—*Hatsell's Precedents of the Proceedings of the House of Commons,* vol. ii. 253. 4to.

advantage; and appointed all the clerks, whose offices became vacant in his time, without any pecuniary consideration whatever. I was the first that experienced the effect of this generosity, as clerk-assistant; to which office I was appointed by Mr. Dyson *, not only without any gratuity on my part, but, indeed, without his having had any personal knowledge of me, till I was introduced to him by Dr. Akenside; and recommended by him as a person, that might be proper to succeed Mr. Reid, then just dead, as clerk-assistant. This office, at the time I received it from Mr. Dyson, 'gratis,' he might have disposed of, and not to an improper person, or one unacquainted with the business of the House of Commons, for 3000*l.* Mr. Dyson's successors, i. e. Mr. Tyrwhitt and myself, have thought ourselves obliged to follow the example which he set; but it is one thing to be the first to refuse a considerable and legal profit, and another, not to resume a practice that has been so honourably abolished by a predecessor †."

The resignation of Mr. Hardinge having introduced Mr. Dyson to that gentleman, Akenside

---

* May 10, 1760.

† Hatsell's Precedents of the House of Commons, vol. ii. 257. 4to.

of men, the next morning, and in a manner quite his own, made a perfect reconcilement, which terminated in a pacific supper, the following night ; when, by a powerful stroke of humour, the host convulsed the sides of his guest with laughter, and they were in delightful unison together, the whole evening. 'Do you kn-kn-know, Doctor,' said he, (for he stammered), ' that I have b-bought a curious pamphlet, this m-morning upon a st-stall, and I'll give you the t-title of it; an acc-count of a curious dispute between D-Dr. Y. and D-Dr. Z , concerning a b-b-bilious c-colic, which brought on a d-duel between the two ph-physicians, which t-terminated in the d-death of both.' "

Shortly after this, Akenside wrote an Ode to his humorous opponent. This ode is not very interesting; but the last stanza points to the ambition, to which the mind of the poet was in perpetual direction.

> " O versed in all the human frame !
>   Lead thou where'er my labour lies,
>   And English fancy's eager flame
>   To Grecian purity chastise ;
>   While, hand in hand, at wisdom's shrine,
>   Beauty with truth I strive to join,

> And grave assent with glad applause,
> To paint the story of the soul,
> And Plato's visions to control
> By Verulamian* laws."

Akenside was particularly partial to inscriptive writing. Mr. Meyrick had two of his copying; and very beautiful ones they are:

" VIBIA . PHRYNE . VIXIT . TER . SENOS . ANNOS
  CARA . MEIS . VIXSI . SVBITO . FATALE . RAPINA
  FLORENTEM . VITA . SVSTVLIT . ATRA . DIES
  HOC . TVMVLO . NVNC . SVM . CINERES . SIMVL . NAMQVE . SA-
      CRATI
  PER . MATREM . CARAM . SVNT . POSITIQVE . MEI
  QVOS . PIVS . SÆPE . COLIT . FRATER . CONIVNXQVE . PVELLÆ
  ATQVE . OBITVM . NOSTRVM . FLETIBVS . USQUE . FLVVNT
  DI . MANES . ME . UNAM . RETINETE . UT . VIVERE . POSSINT
  QVOS . SEMPER . COLUI . VIVA . LIBENTE . ANIMO
  UT . SINT . QVI . CINERES . NOSTROS . BENE . FLORIBUS . SERTIS
  SÆPE . ORNENT . DICAT . SIT . MIHI . TERRA . LEVIS."

" FIRMA EPAPHRODITA.

Ann. xxviii.

FIRMA . SATIS . FELIX . CUM . ME . MEA . VITA . MANERET
  CONJUGIS . OBSEQUIO . CUM . PIETATE . FUI
CONJUGIS . ILLIUS . QUEM . VIX . ACQUARE . MARITI
  ADFECTU . POTERUNT . AUT . BONITATE . PARI

---

* " Verulam gave one of his titles to Francis Bacon, author of the Novum Organum."—A.

G

CONLITERTORUM . VULTUS . ANIMOSQUE . MEORUM
   PLACATOS . MERUI . SEDULITATE . MEA
PLACATOS . MERUI . PER . TE . MAGIS . OMNIS . UT . ALTAS
   SANGUINE . ME . JUNCTAM . CREDERET . ESSE . SIBI
QUI . TECUM . PIA . CASTRA . SEQUI . CONSULTUS . ET . ILLE
   QUEM . LEX . SERVITII . DISTRAHIT . A . DOMINO
HOS . OMNES . TIBI . PRO . MERITIS . QUI . SIDERA . TORQUENT
   SECUM . PLACATOS . SEMPER . HABERE . VELINT."

At what periods Akenside's inscriptions were
written, can only be gathered from the insertion of
them in Dodsley's collection. They have been very
much admired. That on King William exhibits
a pure and classical taste : that for a statue of
Chaucer has a passage of great propriety and
dignity *; that for a column at Runnymede is in
the best style of simplicity; while the one, commemorative of our great dramatic bard, is, perhaps,
the finest specimen of inscriptive poetry in the
English language. That, beginning with

> " Whoe'er thou art, whose path in summer lies
> Through yonder village,"

----

* ———————————" Thou perchance
From Blenheim's towers, O stranger ! Thou art come
Glowing with Churchill's trophies, yet in vain
Dost thou applaud them, if thy breast be cold
To him, this other hero ; who, in times,
Dark and untaught, began with charming voice
To tame the rudeness of his native land."

has a melancholy tale attached to it. This tale is faithfully told in the inscription, and the person, whose memory it preserves, was a young gentleman, who came early into possession of a small estate in the county of Northumberland. I think Sir Grey Cooper, Bart., to whom I shall, hereafter, more particularly allude, said, that his name was Weybridge.

" Whoe'er thou art, whose path in summer lies
   Through yonder village, turn thee where the grove
   Of branching oaks a rural palace old
   Imbosoms. There dwells ALBERT, generous lord
   Of all the harvest round! and onward thence
   A low plain chapel fronts the morning light
   Fast by a silent rivulet. Humbly walk,
   O stranger! o'er the consecrated ground;
   And on that verdant hillock, which thou see'st
   Beset with osiers, let thy pious hand
   Sprinkle fresh water from the brook, and strew
   Sweet-smelling flowers; for there doth EDMUND rest,
   The learned shepherd; for each rural art
   Fam'd, and for songs harmonious, and the woes
   Of ill-requited love. The faithless pride
   Of fair MATILDA sunk him to the grave
   In manhood's prime: but soon did righteous heaven
   With tears, with sharp remorse, and pining care,
   Avenge her falsehood: nor could all the gold,
   And nuptial pomp, which lur'd her plighted faith
   From EDMUND to a loftier husband's house,
   Relieve her broken heart, or turn aside

The strokes of death.   Go, traveller ! relate
The mournful story:—haply some fair maid
May hold it in remembrance, and be taught,
That riches cannot pay for truth or love."

Mr. Dyson was now attending to his duties, as Clerk of the Lower House of Parliament; and Akenside was engaged in making his way as a physician, in the best manner he could; still enjoying the annual income of three hundred pounds, allowed him by his friend: and as it was about this time, that he undertook to rewrite his poem on the Imagination, it is more than probable, that he penned, at this period, his beautiful Invocation: in which, after alluding to the more early scenes of their intimacy, he continues in a strain, worthy the poet to offer, and the friend to accept.

———— " O, my faithful friend !
O early chosen, ever found the same,
 And trusted and beloved !   Once more, the verse
Long destined, always obvious to thine ear,
Attend indulgent: so, in latest years,
When time thy head with honours shall have cloth'd,
Sacred to even virtue, may thy mind,
Amid the calm review of seasons past,
Fair offices of friendship, or kind peace,
Or public zeal:—may then thy mind, well pleas'd,
Recal these happy studies of our prime."
                         P. I. Second Poem, i. v. 87.

About this time, Akenside became a candidate
for the situation of physician to the Charter House;
but his merits were destined to bend before the
good fortune of another, whose sole recommendation
is said to have arisen out of the circumstance of
being related to Lord Holland.   Sir John Hawkins,
who records this, makes a remark upon it, that I
cannot do better than associate with some equally
pertinent observations of Dr. Johnson.   " That a
character, so highly formed as that of Akenside,
should fail of recommending its possessor to those
benefits, which it is in the power of mankind to
bestow, may seem a wonder; but it is often seen,
that negative qualities are more conducive to this
end than positive ; and that, with no higher character than is attainable by any one, who, with a
studious taciturnity, will keep his opinions to himself, conform to the practice of others, and entertain
neither friendship nor enmity against any one, a
competitor for the good opinion of the world, nay
for emoluments, and even dignities, stands a better
chance of success, than one of the most established
reputation for learning and ingenuity." " A physician
in a great city," says Johnson, " seems to be the
mere plaything of fortune ; his degree of reputation
is, for the most part, totally casual: they that employ
him know not his excellence ; they that reject him,

know not his deficience. By any acute observer, who had looked on the transactions of the medical world for half a century, a very curious book might be written on the ' Fortune of Physicians.' "

The practice of Akenside, however, must have been greater than has been generally supposed ; for he kept a carriage. It was obstructed, however, no doubt, by the honesty of his manners, to his dislike of being all things to all men ; and, probably, in a still greater degree by his fame as a poet:—a caprice in direct hostility to the ancient fable, which made Apollo not only god of physic, but of music and poetry.

The manners of Akenside may, perhaps, be illustrated by one of his own alterations. In the first poem he writes

" A purple cloud came floating through the sky."

Book ii. 223.

What can be more natural than this mode of expression? In his MS. notations, however, he alters it to

" Came floating through the sky a purple cloud."

It must be confessed, that if Akenside has sometimes all the grace of Virgil, and all the strength of Lucretius, at others he has all the stiffness and inversion of Callimachus.

We must now enter a little into politics. The

opinions of Akenside and his friend were strongly in favour of the Revolution, and, therefore, in direct harmony with those principles, which placed the family of Brunswick on the throne of Great Britain. His Ode to the Earl of Huntingdon is strongly confirmative of this : there are, therefore, many passages, that could not but give offence to that order of persons, who, out of a puerile reverence of authority, affected to challenge for themselves all loyalty to the sovereign, and all love for the country. I shall quote a passage or two ; as in a future page I shall probably have to refer to them. It may be proper, however, first to recur to a stanza in his ode to SIR FRANCIS HENRY DRAKE; where he predicts the arrival of that period, which soon after came :

" When generous William * was revered,
   Nor one untimely accent heard
   Of James, or his ignoble reign."

---

* His opinion of this monarch flows naturally and gracefully in the following much-admired inscription :—

" GULIELMVS III. FORTIS, PIVS, LIBERATOR, CVM INEVNTE ÆTATE PATRIÆ LATENTI ADFVISSET SALVS IPSE VNICA ; CVM MOX ITIDEM REIPVBLICÆ BRITANNICÆ VINDEX RENVNCIATVS ESSET ATQVE STATOR ; TVM DENIQVE AD ID SE NATVM RECOGNOVIT ET REGEM FACTVM, VT CVRARET NE DOMINO IMPOTENTI CEDERENT PAX, FIDES, FORTVNA, GENERIS HVMANI. AVCTORI PVBLICÆ FELICITATIS. P. G. A. M. A."

The succeeding passage amply testifies his dislike to licence and democracy :

> " Here be it thine to calm and guide
> The swelling democratic tide ;
> To watch the state's uncertain frame,
> And baffle faction's partial aim."
>
> *Ode to E. of H.* v. 2.

But if he was a strenuous adversary to democratic principles, he was equally hostile to those mean, worthless, and degenerate spirits, who combat the friends of freedom not with noble weapons but with disgraceful epithets and ignominious charges. In this manner the enemies of the Revolution endeavoured to stigmatize the Earl of Huntingdon. " Be thou thine own approver !" said Akenside.

> " Be thou thine own approver ! honest praise
> Oft nobly sways
> Ingenuous youth :
> But sought from cowards, and the lying mouth,
> Praise is reproach.   Eternal God alone
> For mortals fixeth that divine award.
> He, from the faithful records of his throne,
> Bids the historian and the bard
> Dispose of honour and of scorn ;
> Discern the patriot from the slave ;
> And write the good, the wise, the brave,
> For lessons to the multitude unborn."

In respect to real, in contra-distinction to licentious liberty, Akenside and Cowper were kindred spirits. .

> " Oh, could I worship aught beneath the skies,
> That earth hath seen, or fancy can devise,
> Thine altar, sacred LIBERTY, should stand,
> Built by no mercenary vulgar hand ;
> With fragrant turf, and flowers as wild and fair,
> As ever dress'd a bank, or scented summer air."

As a lyric poet, Akenside yields, on the whole, to Gray and Collins. He is defective in pathos ; his images occasionally want warmth, and his verse melody ; but his lyrical productions, nevertheless, exhibit a fine glow of sentiment, an ardent admiration of the great and good, an enthusiastic love of true liberty, an utter detestation of tyranny, and a fine sensibility to all the best and noblest feelings of the heart. Dryden's ode is the best adapted to the powers of music ; Collins' Ode of the Passions to dramatic recitation ; and Gray's Bard to excite the sublime aspirations of a Miltonic reader ; —but, next to these, I think there can be no question, that Akenside's Ode to the Earl of Huntingdon is the finest and most powerful lyric poem in the language. In regard to grandeur of sentiment it stands the first.

Akenside was contemporary with a great number

of poets : among whom were Young, Thomson, Armstrong, Glover, Somerville, Sargent, Mallet, and Chatterton; Shenstone, Dyer, and Green; Lyttelton, Collins, Gray, Mason, and Beattie. It does not, however, appear, that he was intimate with any of these poets; and his opinions are, I believe, nowhere upon record, as to their relative merits, except in regard to Dyer's Fleece. "I have been told," says Johnson in his life of Dyer, "that Akenside, who, upon a poetical question, has a right to be heard, said, that he would regulate his opinion of the reigning taste by the fate of Dyer's Fleece; for if that were ill received, he should not think it any longer reasonable to expect fame from excellence."

His opinion in respect to POPE's fourth Epistle on Man is thus recorded by Dr. Warton *:

"Our poet having, in the three former epistles, treated of MAN in all the three respects, in which he can be considered; namely, *first*, of his Nature and State with respect to the Universe; *secondly*, with respect to Himself; *thirdly*, with respect to Society; seems to have finished his subject in the three foregoing Epistles. The fourth Epistle, therefore, on Happiness, may be thought to be adsciti-

* Edition of Pope, vol. ii. 411.

tious, and out of its proper place, and ought to have made part of the second Epistle, where Man is considered with respect to Himself. I formerly mentioned this to Dr. AKENSIDE, and Mr. HARRIS, who were of my opinion."

In another page Dr. Warton records an opinion of Akenside in regard to FENTON's Ode to LORD GOWER: "Akenside frequently said to me, that he thought this ode the best in our language, next to Alexander's Feast *."

I have read this ode; and confess, that I could find only two good stanzas in it.

"Shall Man from Nature's sanction stray,
    With blind Opinion for his guide,
And, rebel to her rightful sway,
    Leave all her bounties unenjoy'd?
Fool! Time no change of Motion knows;
With equal speed the torrent flows,
    To sweep FAME, POWER, and WEALTH away:
        The *past* is all by DEATH possess'd;
        And frugal FATE, that guards the rest,
By giving, bids him live *to-day*."

*   *   *   *   *

"O GOWER! Through all that destined space,
    What breath the Powers allot to me,
Shall sing the virtues of thy race,
    United and complete in thee.

---

* Edition of Pope. vol. ii. 401.

O flower of ancient English faith !
Pursue th' unbeaten Patriot-path,
    In which, confirm'd, thy father shone :
The light, his fair example gives,
Already from thy dawn receives
    A lustre equal to its own."

Akenside's critical judgment seems to have been
greatly respected by his cotemporaries.   " His comments," says the Hon. George Hardinge, in a letter
to Mr. Nichols, " were cherished by those book-
sellers, who lent him new books; and if any one
struck him with a powerful impression, I believe it
was generally given to him by the publisher."   His
judgment is, also, appealed to in a very favourable
manner by Dr. Warton :

" By the favour of Dr. LOWTH, the late excellent Bishop of London, I have seen a copy of
SPENCE's Essay on the Odyssey, with marginal
observations written in Pope's own hand, and generally acknowledging the justice of Spence's observations; and in a few instances pleading, humorously
enough, that some favourite lines might be spared.
I speak from experience, when I say, that I know
no critical treatise better calculated to form the
taste of young men of genius, than this Essay on
the Odyssey.   And lest it should be thought that
this opinion arises from my partiality to a friend,

with whom I lived so many years in the happiest
intimacy, I will add, that this also was the opinion
of three persons, from whose judgment there can be
no appeal, Dr. AKENSIDE, Bishop LOWTH, and Mr.
JAMES HARRIS."

And here we may with propriety introduce, on
the authority of ISAAC REED, Esq. another paper,
written by Akenside, published in Dodsley's Museum. It is entitled the BALANCE OF POETS; and
can be considered in no other light than as a very
curious and important paper, coming, as it does,
from so accomplished a person. It may not, however, be presumptuous to hint, that all critics will,
perhaps, not feel disposed to coincide with his decisions.

THE BALANCE OF POETS.

M. DE PILES is one of the most judicious authors
on the art of Painting. He has added to his treatise on
that subject a very curious paper, which he calls the
Balance of the Painters. He divides the whole art of
painting into four heads : composition, design, colouring, and expression ; under each of which he assigns
the degree of perfection, which the several masters have
obtained. To this end he first settles the degree of
sovereign perfection, which has never been attained,

and which is beyond even the taste or knowledge of
the best critics at present : this he rates as the twen-
tieth degree.   The nineteenth degree is the highest of
which the human mind has any comprehension ; but
which has not yet been expressed or executed by the
greatest masters.   The eighteenth is that to which the
greatest masters have actually attained ; and so down-
wards, according to their comparative genius and skill.
Monsieur de Piles makes four columns of his four chief
articles or parts of painting ; and opposite to the names
of the great masters, unites their several degrees of perfection in each article.   The thought is very ingenious ;
and had it been executed with accuracy, and a just
rigour of taste, would have been of the greatest use to
the lovers of that noble art.   But we can hardly expect,
that any man should be exactly right in his judgment,
through such a multiplicity of the most delicate ideas.

I have often wished to see a balance of this kind,
that might help to settle our comparative esteem of the
greater POETS in the several polite languages.   But as
I have never seen nor heard of any such design, I have
here attempted it myself, according to the best information which my private taste could afford me.   I shall
be extremely glad, if any of your ingenious corre-
spondents will correct me where I am wrong ; and in
the meantime shall explain the general foundations of
my scheme, where it differs from that of the French
author.   For he has not taken in a sufficient number of
articles to form a complete judgment of the art of painting ; and though he had, yet poetry requires many more.

I shall retain his numbers, and suppose twenty to be the degree of absolute perfection, and eighteen the highest, that any poet has attained.

His first article is COMPOSITION; in which his balance is quite equivocal and uncertain. For there are, in painting, two sorts of composition, utterly different from each other. One relates to the eye, the other to the passions: so that the former may be not improperly styled *picturesque* composition, and is concerned only with such a disposition of the figures, as may render the whole group of the picture entire and well united; the latter is concerned with such attitudes and connexions of the figures, as may effectually touch the passions of the spectator. There are, in poetry, two analogous kinds of composition or ordonnance; one of which belongs to the general plan or structure of the work, and is an object of the cool judgment of a connoisseur; the other relates to the most striking situations, and the most moving incidents. And though these are most strictly connected in truth and in the principles of art, yet, in fact, we see them very frequently disjoined; and they depend indeed on different powers of the mind. SIR RICHARD BLACKMORE, a name for contempt, or for oblivion, in the commonwealth of poetry, had more of the former than SHAKESPEARE; who had more of the latter than any man, that ever lived. The former we shall call *Critical Ordonnance*, the latter *Pathetic;* and these make the two first columns of our balance.

It may, perhaps, be necessary to observe here, that though, literally speaking, these two articles relate only to epic and dramatic poetry; yet we shall apply them to every other species. For in lyric poetry, in satire, in comedy, in the ethical epistle, one author may excel another in the general plan and disposition of his work ; and yet fall short of him in the arguments, allusions, and other circumstances, which he employs to move his reader, and to obtain the end of his particular composition.

Our next article answers to that which Monsieur de Piles calls EXPRESSION ; but this, likewise, in poetry, requires two columns. Painting represents only a single instant of time ; consequently it expresses only a present passion, without giving any idea of the general character or turn of mind. For poetry expresses this part as well as the other ; and the same poet is not equally excellent in both. Homer far surpasses Virgil in the general delineation of characters and manners ; but there are, in Virgil, some expressions of particular passions, greatly superior to any in Homer. I shall, therefore, divide this head of expression, and call the former *Dramatic Expression*, and the latter *Incidental*.

Our next article answers to what the painters call DESIGN, or the purity, beauty, and grandeur of the outline in drawing ; to which the taste of beauty in description, and the truth of expression, are analogous in poetry. But as the term design, except among painters, is generally supposed to mean the general plan and contrivance of a work, I shall therefore omit it, to prevent mistakes; and substitute instead of it, *the Truth of Taste*, by which to distinguish the fifth column. And indeed, this article would likewise admit of several subdivisions; for some poets are excellent for the grandeur of their

taste, others for its beauty, and others for a kind of
neatness. But they may all be ranged under the same
head; as MICHAEL ANGELO, RAPHAEL, and POUSSIN,
are all characterised from their design. The truth of
taste will, cæteris paribus, belong to the first in the
highest degree; but we must always remember, that
there can be no greatness without justness and decorum;
which is the reason that RAPHAEL is counted higher
in design than MICHAEL ANGELO. For though this
latter had a grandeur and more masculine taste, yet
RAPHAEL, with a truly grand one, was incomparably
more correct and true.

It is not easy to assign that part of poetry, which
answers to the colouring of a painter. A very good
judge of painting calls the COLOURING the procuress
of her sister, DESIGN; who gains admirers for her,
that otherwise might not, perhaps, be captivated with
her charms. If we trace this idea through poetry, we
shall, perhaps, determine poetical colouring to be such a
general choice of words, such an order of grammatical
construction, and such a movement and turn of the
verse, as are most favourable to the poet's invention,
distinct from the ideas which those words convey. For
whoever has reflected much on the pleasure which
poetry communicates, will recollect many words which,
taken singly, excite very similar ideas; but which have
very different effects, according to their situation and
connexion in a period. It is impossible to read Virgil,
but especially Milton, without making this observation
a thousand times. The sixth column of the balance
shall, therefore, be named from this poetical colouring.

H

As for VERSIFICATION, its greatest merit is always provided for by the last article; but as it would seem strange to many, should we entirely omit it; the seventh column shall, therefore, be allotted for it as far as it relates to the mere harmony of sound.

The eighth article belongs to the MORAL of the several poets, or to the truth and merit of the sentiments which they express, or the dispositions which they inculcate with respect to religion, civil society, or private life. The reader must not be surprised, if he find the heathen poets not so much degraded, as he might expect in this particular; for though their representations of Divine Providence be so absurd and shocking, yet this article is intended to characterise the comparative goodness of their moral intention, and not the comparative soundness of their speculative opinions. *Where little is given, little is required.*

The ninth and last column contains an ESTIMATE of their comparative value and eminence upon the whole. This is greatly wanting in the French author. The degrees of perfection, which he assigns to RUBENS, make up a sum, when the four articles are added to each other, exactly equal to what he calculates for Raphael; so that one, not greatly versed in the study of pictures, might imagine from thence that Rubens was as great a painter as Raphael. This general estimate is also more necessary in the present scheme, as some of the articles, particularly that of Ordonnance, are applied equally to every species of poetry; so that a Satirist will be rated as high, in that article, as an Epic poet; provided his Ordonnance be as perfect for satire, as that of the other is for heroic poetry. Upon this account, justice to the manes of the divine poets requires, that we should acknowledge their pre-eminence upon the whole, after having thus set their inferiors upon a level with them in particular parts.

You see this general method is here applied to a few, the greater names of poetry in most polite languages. I have avoided to bring in any living authors, because I know the vanity and emulation of the poetical tribe; which I mention, lest the reader may find fault with me for omitting Voltaire, Metastasio, or any favourite author of our own nation.

	Critical Ordonnance.	Pathetic Ordonnance.	Dramatic Expression.	Incidental Expression.	Taste.	Colouring.	Versification.	Moral.	Final Estimate.
Ariosto . .	—	15	10	15	14	15	16	10	13
Boileau . .	18	16	12	14	17	14	13	16	12
Cervantes .	17	17	15	17	12	16	—	16	14
Corneille .	15	16	16	16	16	14	12	16	14
Dante . .	12	15	8	17	12	15	14	14	13
Euripides .	15	16	14	17	13	14	—	15	12
Homer . .	18	17	18	15	16	16	18	17	18
Horace . .	12	12	10	16	17	17	16	14	13
Lucretius .	14	5	—	17	17	14	16	—	10
Milton . .	17	15	15	17	18	18	17	18	17
Moliere .	15	17	17	17	15	16	—	16	14
Pindar . .	10	10	—	17	17	16	—	17	13
Pope . .	16	17	12	17	16	15	15	17	13
Racine . .	17	16	15	15	17	13	12	15	13
Shakspeare	—	18	18	18	10	17	10	18	18
Sophocles .	18	16	15	15	16	14	—	16	13
Spenser . .	8	15	10	16	17	17	17	17	14
Tasso . .	17	14	14	13	12	13	16	13	12
Terence .	18	12	10	12	17	14	—	16	10
Virgil . .	17	10	17	17	18	17	17	17	16

The estimate stands thus:

CRITICAL ORDONNANCE.

First Class. * Homer, Sophocles, Terence, Boileau.
Second   .   Virgil, Tasso, Milton, Racine.
Third   .   Pope.
Fourth   .   Euripides, Corneille.
Fifth   .   Lucretius.
Sixth   .   Horace, Dante.
Seventh   .   Pindar.
Eighth   .   Spenser.

Ariosto and Shakspeare disdained critical ordonnances.

PATHETIC ORDONNANCE.

First Class.   Shakspeare.
Second   .   Homer.
Third   .   Sophocles, Euripides, Corneille, Racine.
Fourth   .   Dante, Ariosto, Spenser, Milton.
Fifth   .   Tasso.
Sixth   .   Terence, Horace.
Seventh   .   Pindar, Virgil.

DRAMATIC EXPRESSION.

First Class.   Homer and Shakspeare.
Second   .   Virgil.
Third   .   Corneille.
Fourth   .   Sophocles, Milton, Racine.

---

* The reader is requested to observe, that each poet is placed in the following summaries, according to the only order the author's arrangement admits of, viz. a chronological one.

Fifth	.	Euripides, Tasso.
Sixth	.	Boileau, Pope.
Seventh	.	Terence, Horace, Ariosto, Spenser.

INCIDENTAL EXPRESSION.

First Class.		Shakspeare.
Second	.	Euripides, Pindar, Lucretius, Virgil, Dante, Milton, Pope.
Third	.	Horace, Spenser, Corneille.
Fourth	.	Homer, Sophocles, Ariosto, Racine.
Fifth	.	Boileau.
Sixth	.	Tasso.
Seventh	.	Terence.

TASTE.

First Class.		Virgil, Milton.
Second	.	Pindar, Terence, Lucretius, Horace, Spenser, Boileau, Racine.
Third	.	Homer, Sophocles, Corneille, Pope.
Fourth	.	Ariosto.
Fifth	.	Euripides.
Sixth	.	Dante and Tasso.
Seventh	.	Shakspeare.

COLOURING.

First Class.		Milton.
Second	.	Virgil, Horace, Shakspeare, Spenser.
Third	.	Homer, Pindar.
Fourth	.	Dante, Ariosto, Pope.
Fifth	.	Euripides, Sophocles, Terence, Lucretius, Corneille, Boileau.
Sixth	.	Tasso, Racine.

We may now quote two FRAGMENTS from the pages of Dr. Warton, illustrative of Akenside's

---

thing of the *clinquant* of Tasso : and the magic of this word, like the report of Astolfo's horn in Ariosto, overturned at once the solid and well-built reputation of the Italian poetry.

" It is not, perhaps, strange, that this potent word should do its business in France. What was less to be expected, it put us into a fright on this side the water. Mr. Addison, who gave the law in taste here, took it up, and sent it about the kingdom in his polite and popular Essays *. It became a sort of watchword among the critics ; and, on the sudden, nothing was heard, on all sides, but the *clinquant* of Tasso."

It is curious to observe the presumption of some men, even eminent men—as BOILEAU must certainly be allowed to have been ; though not a great one. MAFFEI lets out a secret, in respect to him ; for he assures us, that Racine's elder son told him, that Boileau had not only never read Tasso, but that he knew scarcely one word of Italian.

I cannot but say, that I think Akenside was in some degree deficient in that language also. Had he dipt deeply into that holy fountain, he would, perhaps, in common with Milton, have discovered that Tasso's metal was not *tinsel,* but solid *gold.* He would, also, I think, out of regard to so excellent a man, and so lofty a genius, have passed over that part of the poet's life, wherein " his poverty, rather than his will," consented. " *Pardone,*" said he, in a letter to a friend, " *a me quest ardimento di lodar me stesso, poichè io agevol- mente lo perdonata l'importunita d'aver lodati molti contra mia voglia, e contra il proprio giudicio.*"

---

* Spectator, vol. i. No. 5. ; vol. v. No. 369.

opinions in regard to correctness of writing; and the inadequacy of the French language to the expression of poetical ideas. Warton seems to have quoted from the conversation of Akenside. At least, I do not recollect in what book or paper, except in his edition of Pope, the following sentiments are to be found.

" 'Tis hard," said AKENSIDE, " to conceive by what means the French acquired the character of superior correctness. We have classic authors in English, older than in any modern language, except the Italian; and Spenser and Sidney wrote with the truest taste, when the French had not one great poet they can bear to read. Milton and Chapelin were contemporaries; the Pucelle

---

In a book, printed in black-letter, 1588, entitled *The Householder's Philosophie*, and said to be translated from the Italian of that " *excellent orator and poet,* SIGNIOR TORQUATO TASSO," we have these words:—

" 𝕸any are serbants by fortune, that are free by nature. And it is not to be marbailled at, that many cruell conflicts and daungerous warres are caused and continued by such as these. Howbeit it is a great argument of baseness, that seruile fortune can engender seruile euils in a gentle mind." Fol. 15.

This book I take to be an imposition. I see nothing, assimilating with the subject, in any of the general collections of Tasso's works; but the coincidence of sentiment is remarkable.

and Paradise Lost were in hand, perhaps frequently, at the self-same hour.   One of them was executed in such a manner, that an Athenian of Menander's age would have turned his eyes from the Minerva of Phidias, or the Venus of Apelles, to obtain more perfect conceptions of beauty from the English poet; the other, though fostered by the French court for twenty years with the utmost indulgence, does honour to the Leonine and the Runic poetry.   It was too great an attention to French criticism, that hindered her poets, in Charles the Second's time, from comprehending the genius and acknowledging the authority of Milton; else, without looking abroad, they might have acquired a manner more correct and perfect, than French authors could, or can teach them."

———————

" Were I a Frenchman," said AKENSIDE, " concerned for the poetical glory of my country, I should lament its unmusical language, and the impossibility of forming it to numbers or harmony.   The French ode is an uncertain mixture of different feet, changing at random the rhythmus or movement of the verse, and disappointing one's ear, just as if a dancer in the midst of a minuet should fall a capering in the harlequin step, or break out into a Lancashire hornpipe.   Their Alexandrine measure, which they call heroic, has its pause or cæsura in every line in the same place; so that two hammers make just as much music as Racine or Boileau. If this be without remedy in the French language, their language is very unfortunate for Poetry; but it is diverting to hear these finished critics and masters of correctness valuing themselves upon this wretched, unmusical poverty in their verse, and blaming the licentiousness of English poetry ; because it allows a variation of the pause, and a suspension of the period from one verse into any part of another ; without which poetry has less harmony than prose."

We may now introduce Akenside's confession of the love and admiration, he always entertained for Greek learning, manners, and sentiments ; and, for the greater variety, we shall adopt the version of the Italian translator.

> " Genio di Grecia, se non tardo i' tenni
> L'orme tue fide sul difficil calle
> Di Natura, e Scienza alme nudrici
> De' bei desiri, e dell' eroiche gesta ;
> Fa che nell' aura di tua lode il mio
> Petto s' infiammi ad adeguar l' eccelso
> Non tentato argomento ; e non fia mai,
> Che di baldanza alcun m' accusi e adonti,
> Se nell' ore tranquille d'una sera,
> Cui pinge April di lusinghevol riso,
> Fuggo sdegnoso il sordido ricetto
> Di vile ambizion, del garrir vano,
> Impaziente di seguirti, o sacro
> Nume, per le silvestri ombre romite
> Dal loro infesto piè non tocche ancora.
> Scendi, O Genio propizio," .&c.
>
> MAZZA, I. 721.

Akenside seems to have been a great friend to Dodsley's Miscellany; for he occasionally recommended papers for insertion in it. Among those, thus recommended, was Welsted's Ode on the Duke of Marlborough *.

Welsted was an acquaintance of Akenside; but in what estimation he was held, we are not informed. He had a place in the Ordnance office, and a house in the Tower. His great patron was the Duke of Newcastle, and Warburton asserts, that he received five hundred pounds from the secret service fund for writing anonymously in behalf of the ministry, of which his grace was a member. He was author of a comedy, acted in 1726 in Lincoln's-Inn-Fields, with some success, entitled " *The Dissembled Woman ; or, My Son get Money* †." He wrote, also, in early life, a satire against Pope, called " The Triumvirate ;" for which that poet punished him with a parody in the Dunciad.

" Flow, WELSTED, flow! like thine inspirer, Beer,
        Though stale, not ripe; though thin,.yet never clear;

---

* Warton.

† This comedy is supposed to be alluded to in No. 182 of the Tatler.

So sweetly mawkish, and so smoothly dull ;
Heady, not strong ; o'erflowing, though not full *."

---

* Dunciad, III. 169.   Pope names him also in his Pro-
logue to the Satires:

" Three thousand suns went down on Welsted's lie."

" This man had the impudence to tell in print, that
Mr. P. had occasioned a *lady's death,* and to name a person,
he never heard of.   He also published, that he libelled the
Duke of Chandos; with whom (it was added) that he lived
in familiarity, and received from him a present of *five hundred pounds:* the falsehood of both which is known to his
grace.   Mr. P. never received any present, farther than the
subscription for Homer, from him, or from any great man
whatever."—P.

Welsted published a translation of Longinus' treatise " On
the Sublime."   He gave out, that he translated it from the
Greek ; but the fact was, it was no other than a translation
from the French of Boileau.   He dedicated it to the Bishop
of Winchester.

He was, also, author of a book (which he inscribed to the
DUKE of CHANDOS,) entitled " *The Scheme and Conduct of
Providence.*"   This consists of observations on that law of
the decalogue, which threatens punishment to sons for the
crimes of their fathers.

As a poet, he had some reputation in his day.   The following specimen is from his SUMMUM BONUM.

To his great chiefs the conqueror PYRRHUS spoke,
" Two moons shall wane, and Greece shall own our yoke."
" 'Tis well," replied the friend : " admit it so,
What next?"   " Why next to Italy I 'll go,

In 1749, a company of French Comedians were acting in London by subscription. A part of the public were very indignant at this circumstance; and Akenside partook of it. But to refuse to listen to the French Drama, because France is our rival, were not only unjust and impolitic; but absurd, and even ridiculous. Akenside, however, thought otherwise; and, in consequence, wrote what he called the REMONSTRANCE of SHAKSPEARE. As a whole, it is, perhaps, unworthy of the author's genius; but there is some point in the lines, in which he characterizes the French Drama.

> " Say, does your humble admiration choose
> The gentle prattle of her comic muse;
> While wits, plain-dealers, fops, and fools, appear,
> Charged to say nought but what the king may hear?
> Or rather, melts your sympathizing hearts,
> Won by her tragic scenes' romantic arts,
> Where old and young declaim on soft desire,
> And heroes never but for love expire?"

And Rome in ashes lay."   " What after that?"
" Waste India's realms."   " What then?"   " Then sit and
      chat;
Then quaff the grape, and mirthful stories tell."
" Sir, you may do so now, and full as well."

Welsted died in 1747.

In 1750, Akenside wrote an Ode to WILLIAM
HALL, ESQ. of the Middle Temple.   Mr. Hall
was an intimate friend of Markland, who inscribed
to him his *Quæstio Grammatica.* He ranked, also,
among his friends, Lord Jersey, Lord Clarendon,
Lord Hampden, and the first Lord Camden.   His
manners partook of the society he had kept; he
had a good person, and a pleasing countenance.
He was, besides, a man not only gifted with a fine
taste in subjects of art and literature; but he was
a poet of no mean order.   His translation from
Anacreon* is universally known; and the following sonnet to Mr. Nicholas Hardinge, on the first
impression of Lauder's Forgeries, reminds us of
several sonnets, written by the poet, that he celebrates.

" HARDINGE †! firm advocate of Milton's fame!
  Avenge the honour of his injured muse!
  The bold SALMASIUS dared not so accuse,
And brand him, living, with a felon's name!

---

* In the dead of the night, when with labour opprest,
  All mortals enjoy the sweet blessings of rest,
  A boy knock'd at my door, &c. &c.

† Mr. Nicholas Hardinge was a very able critic, and was
the first who gave the true reading in a remarkable passage

Arch-forger, cursed poison to infuse
In Eve's chaste ear, her freedom to abuse:
That lurking fiend,—Ithuriel's arm and flame,
Ætherial gifts detected: but this plot
Thou hast an arm, and spear, that can expose;
With lashes keen, drive, to that traitorous spot,
The nurse of base impostors, to his snows,
And barren mountains, the blaspheming Scot!"

---

in one of Horace's Odes. Dr. Bentley was struck with it, and passed a very high but singular commendation of it, characteristic of his own pedantry and wit. A whimsical appeal was made to him, when he was clerk of the House of Commons: Pulteney and Sir Robert Walpole were squabbling; and the former playfully told the latter, that his *Latin* was as bad as his *politics*. He had quoted a line from Horace*, and Pulteney insisted that he had *misquoted* it. The other would not give it up. A guinea was laid, and Mr. Hardinge was the arbiter; who rose with a very droll solemnity, and gave it against his own patron, Sir Robert. The guinea was thrown across the house, which Pulteney took up, saying, it was " the *first public money that he had touched for a long time.*" He had formerly been in office. It should be added, to make the anecdote complete, that at Pulteney's death, the individual guinea was found, wrapped up in a piece of paper, with a memorandum upon it, recording the circumstance.—*Nichols.*

---

* ————— " His murus aheneus esto
Nil conscire sibi, *nulla* pallescere *culpâ.*"

Sir Robert repeated it, " *nulli* pallescere *culpæ.*"

In spite, however, of all the elegances, by which Mr. Hall was distinguished, there was one passion, to which he was most culpably devoted—the love of women: and it was this passion, that induced Akenside to address him with an ode, accompanied with the poems of DE CHAULIEU, whom he seems to have, in some respects, resembled *.

* The Abbé de Chaulieu was born at his father's seat at Fontenai, in the Vexen-Normand, in 1639. An excellent education, joined with quick natural parts, and an easy gaiety of disposition, soon rendered him the delight of elegant society, and in particular gained him the friendship of the great Duke of Vendome, and his brother, the grandprior of Malta. They treated him with familiarity, and gave him the management of their affairs, which they repaid with several benefiçes of considerable value. He, also, possessed the Lordship of Fontenai; so that he was enabled to follow at his ease the pleasurable life, to which he was addicted. His apartments at the Temple, in Paris, were the resort of a society of lettered friends, whom he charmed by the liveliness of his conversation, and the amiable qualities of his heart.

The poetry, by which Chaulieu distinguished himself, is a mixture of the voluptuous and sentimental, partaking of the gaiety of Anacreon, and the philosophical good-humour of Horace. He was the poetical pupil of Chapelle, whom he imitated in the easy negligence of his verse, and the occasional use of double rhymes. Though he was superior to what Pope has denominated " the mob of gentlemen, who write with ease;" yet he is rather to be classed with the careless

In this Ode, the poet condemns the licentiousness of Chaulieu; but he makes a concession, to
which it is impossible to accede.

> " We own, had Fate to man assign'd
>   Nor sense, nor wish, but what obey
>   Or Venus soft or Bacchus gay ;
> Then might our bard's voluptuous creed
> Most aptless govern human-kind :
>   Unless, perchance, what he hath sung
>   Of tortur'd joints and nerves unstrung,
> Some wrangling heretic should plead."

Akenside seems, for a moment, to forget, that
temperance must, in all cases, be the best luxury ;
and that wisdom and virtue are the best rewards.

men of genius, than with the masters of the art.   Voltaire,
in his " Temple of Taste," has thus characterized him :

> Je vis arriver en ce lieu
> Le brillant Abbe de Chaulieu,
> Qui chantoit en sortant de table.
> Il osoit caresser le Dieu
> D'un air familier, mais aimable.
> Sa vive imagination
> Prodiguoit, dans sa douce ivresse,
> Des beautés sans correction,
> Qui chocquoient un peu la justesse,
> Et respiroient la passion.

This Epicurean, notwithstanding frequent attacks of the
gout, lived to his 81st year; dying at Paris in 1720.—
Aikin from Moreri.

In 1766, Mr. Hall retired to Bath, to take the benefit of the waters, and there fell into a state, says the Hon. George Hardinge, perhaps unexampled in the philosophy of human decay. "He became first weak, then childish; and from that idiotcy emerged into the wildest paroxysm of delirium, in which he died *."

Akenside had been some time acquainted with the celebrated CHARLES TOWNSEND, brother of the first Marquis of Townsend; one of the best parliamentary speakers of his time †; in 1754 a Lord

---

* December, 1766.

† His oratorical powers are thus described by Mr. Burke. " You understand, that I speak of Charles Townsend, whom I cannot even now remember without some degree of sensibility. In truth, he was the delight and ornament of this house, and the charm of every private society which he honoured with his presence. Perhaps there never arose in this country, nor in any country, a man of a more pointed and finished wit; and (where his passions were not concerned) of a more refined, exquisite, and penetrating judgment. If he had not so great a stock, as some have had, who flourished formerly, of knowledge, long treasured up, he knew better by far, than any man I ever was acquainted with, how to bring together in a short time, all that was necessary to establish, to illustrate, and to decorate that side of the question he supported. He stated his matter skilfully and powerfully. He particularly excelled in a most luminous explanation and display of his subject. His style of argu-

of the Admiralty, and, subsequently, Chancellor of the Exchequer.

To this eminent person, who was, no doubt, one of Akenside's patients *, the poet addressed two Odes. The first is not distinguished by any passage of interest, if we except the allusions to the affliction, with which the poet had been visited on the loss of Olympia. The second seems to have

ment was neither trite and vulgar, nor subtle and abstruse. He hit the house just between wind and tide. And not being troubled with too anxious a zeal for any matter in question, he was never tedious, or more earnest, than the preconceived opinions and present temper of the house; and he seemed to guide, because he was always sure to follow it.

" There are many young members in the house (such, of late, has been the rapid succession of public men), who never saw that prodigy, Charles Townsend ; nor of course know what a ferment he was able to excite in every thing by the violent ebullition of his mixed virtues and failings,—for failings he had undoubtedly—many of us remember them— we are this day considering the effect of them. But he had no failings, which were not owing to a noble cause; to an ardent, generous, perhaps an immoderate passion for fame; a passion, which is the instinct of all great souls."

> * " Oh ! knew'st thou how the balmy air,
>   The sun, the azure heav'ns, prepare
>   To heal thy languid frame ;
>   No more would noisy courts engage,
>   In vain would lying faction's rage
>   Thy sacred leisure claim."

been written while he was upon a visit to Mr.
Townsend in the country; and, like the ode to the
Earl of Huntingdon, breathes all that an Englishman can desire. Their friendship was, however, at
last dissolved.

Johnson endeavoured to explain this friendship
on grounds, not justified by the premises. " Sir,"
said he to Boswell, " a man is very apt to complain
of the ingratitude of those, who have risen far above
him. A man, when he gets into a higher sphere,
into other habits of life, cannot keep up all his
former connexions. Then, sir, those who knew
him formerly, upon a level with themselves, may
think they ought to be treated as on a level, which
cannot be. An acquaintance in a former situation
may bring out things, which would be very disagreeable to have mentioned before higher company;
though, perhaps, every body knows of them. This
dissolved the friendship of Akenside and Charles
Townsend." But this is no appropriate instance,
as Mr. Croker justly observes in his late comprehensive edition of Boswell's Life of Johnson.
" Charles Townsend, the nephew of the Prime
Minister, the son of a peer, who was Secretary of
State, and leader of the House of Commons, was as
much above Akenside in their earliest days, as at

any subsequent period. Nor was Akenside in rank inferior to Dr. Brocklesby, with whom Charles Townsend continued in intimate friendship, to the end of his life."

In 1751 appeared a work, under the title of *"Memoires pour servir à l'Histoire de la Maison de Brandebourg."* This work, being written by Frederic, king of Prussia, was universally read throughout Europe. It contained many extraordinary passages, and among the rest the two following :—

" Il se fit une migration (the author is speaking of what happened of the Revocation of Nantz *), *dont on n'avoit guère vu d'exemples dans l'histoire : un peuple entier sortit du royaume par l'esprit de parti en haine du pape, et pour recevoir sous un autre ciel la communion sous les deux espèces : quatre cens mille ames s'expatrierent ainsi et abandonnerent tous leur biens pour detonner dans d'autres temples les vieux pseaumes de Clement Marot."*

" La crainte donna le jour à la crédulité, et l'amour propre interessa bientôt le ciel au destin des hommes."

Perceiving the consequences of these passages on the minds of the ignorant;—more especially since they proceeded from so high a quarter,—Akenside wrote an ode to the author. This ode has nothing

* M. A.

very remarkable; but there is one stanza, and that a very fine one, which we may quote, because it respects not only the general argument, but another, he had assumed in his " Pleasures of Imagination;" viz. that ridicule is the test of truth.

> "O evil foresight, and pernicious care!
> Wilt thou indeed abide by this appeal?
> Shall we the lessons of thy pen compare
> With private honour, or with public zeal?
> Whence, then, at things divine those darts of scorn?
> Why are the woes, which virtuous men have borne
> For sacred truth, a prey to laughter given?
> What fiend, what foe of nature, urged thy arm
> Th' Almighty of his sceptre to disarm,
> To push this earth adrift, and leave it loose from Heav'n?"

Three years after, following the same course, Akenside wrote an ode to the truly admirable Hoadley, Bishop of Winchester; an excellent man, a constitutional politician, and a truly Christian bishop. He had been, successively, Bishop of Bangor, Hereford, and Salisbury; and having long been actively engaged in the endeavour to awaken and keep alive a regard to civil and political liberty, Akenside's ode operated not only as a farther excitement, but as a reward: for the virtues of the bishop are celebrated in the best manner; and his

principles recommended to the observance and preservation of all after times *.

In July, 1755, Akenside read the Gulstonian
Lectures before the College of Physicians. In these
lectures, he advanced opinions, relative to the
lymphatic vessels of animals, in decisive opposition
to those of Boerhaave. These opinions may be
gathered from the following abstract. " That the
lymphatics in general have their origin among the
little cavities of the cellular substance of the muscles,
among the mucous solliculi of the tendons, or the
membranous receptacles and ducts of the larger
glands:—that their extremities or roots imbibe from
these cavities the moisture, exhaled there from the
ultimate arterial tubes, just as the lacteals, which
are the lymphatics of the mesentery, do on the concave surface of the intestines ; and that the minute
imbibing vessels, by gradually opening one into
another, form, at length, a lymphatic trunk, furnished with valves to prevent the return of its fluid,
and tending uniformly from the extremities and
from the viscera, to reconvey to the blood that

---

* Bishop Hoadley was frequently styled by his adversaries,
the REPUBLICAN BISHOP ; but the learned and admirable
Lowth, in his Life of Wickham, calls him " the great advocate of civil and religious liberty."

lymph, or that fine steam, with which they are kept
in perpetual moisture; a circumstance indispensable
to life and motion; while, at the same time, the
continual re-absorption of that moisture, by the
lymphatics, is no less necessary to preserve the
blood properly fluid, and to prevent the putrefac-
tion, which would inevitably follow, if this animal
vapour were suffered to stagnate in the cavities,
where it is discharged."

This theory, Akenside asserts, he drew out for
himself; and before the delivery of which before
the College of Surgeons, no public mention had
been made. These observations, he goes on to
assure us, he did not print at the time. But a dispute having, afterwards, arisen between two other
gentlemen, who each claimed for himself the honour
of the discovery, Akenside was prevailed upon to
give in, at a meeting of the Royal Society, so much
of his lectures, as related to the subject in question.
This portion of the lectures was, in consequence,
laid before the Royal Society; and it being read
in the presence of several gentlemen, who had,
formerly, heard the lectures themselves, the paper
was published in the Philosophical Transactions by
the Council of the Royal Society. It was, therefore, with no small surprise and indignation, that

Akenside learnt, some time after, that Dr. Alexander Munro, Professor of Anatomy at Edinburgh, had published some Remarks, in a Postscript to a Pamphlet, entitled Observations, Anatomical and Physiological; insinuating, that Akenside did not discover his conjecture, relative to the lymphatic vessels of animals, until Dr. Monro's Treatise on the same lymphatics had been sent to England.

Akenside's observations had been addressed to the College of Surgeons in 1755. The publication of them took place in 1757; Dr. Monro's Treatise arrived in England in 1756. It was impossible, therefore, that Akenside could have taken the idea from Dr. Monro, as the statement of the latter implied:—But had the observations been printed in the Philosophical Transactions, without any testimony to prove, that they had been previously read before the College of Surgeons, Akenside would have had no small trouble to convince the world, that he was indeed the original discoverer. The memory of Akenside has been, in fact, strangely neglected by medical men; and it will give me great pleasure, should these pages become the humble instrument of his being, hereafter, more adequately appreciated.

I think it probable, that what was said of Dr.

Garth might be, with equal justice, applied to Dr. Akenside; viz.—that no physician knew his art more, nor his trade less *.

The year 1757 is remarkable in the life of Akenside, for his having completed the first book of his second poem on the Pleasures of the Imagination.

In 1758 he wrote his Ode to the Country Gentlemen of England. The poet-laureate, WHITEHEAD, also published " verses to the people of England," at the same time; in the same form; and at the same price †.

" This ode," says Mr. Justice Hardinge, in a

* " Garth was a man," says Warton ‡, " of the sweetest disposition, amiable manners, and universal benevolence; all parties, at a time when party violence was at a great height, joined in praising and loving him." And here I cannot deny myself the pleasure of quoting Pope's opinion of the physicians of his time.

" There is no end of my kind treatment from the faculty," said he, in a letter to Mr. Allen a few weeks before he died. " *They are, in general, the most amiable companions, and the best friends, as well as most learned men I know.*" He can have but a very limited knowledge of society, who cannot apply this to the medical men of the present age, as well as to that which is passed.

† Quarto, sixpence.

‡ Ed. of Pope, Vol. I. p. 75.

letter to Mr. Nichols, "is unequal; but it has glorious passages in it.   Mr. Elliott, father of Lord Minto, made an admirable speech in support of the Scotch militia, which I had the good fortune to hear, when I was a boy : and it was reported, that when commended, as he was, on every side, for that performance ;—' If I was above myself,' answered he, ' I can account for it ; for I had been animated by the sublime ode of Dr. Akenside.'"

The criticisms of cotemporaries on eminent literary characters are of little authority, while those characters are living; but they become interesting in the distant time.   With this impression I insert a criticism on this poem, from the Monthly Review. " The poetical productions of this twofold disciple of Apollo " have this peculiar excellence ;   they

---

* This title was first given to Akenside in Cooper's Call of Aristippus.

> " O thou, for whom the British bays
>   Bloom in these unpoetic days,
> Whose early genius glow'd to follow
>   The arts through Nature's ancient ways,
> *Two-fold disciple of Apollo !*
>
>   Shall Aristippus' easy lays,
>   Trifles of philosophic pleasure,
>   Composed in literary leisure,
>   Aspire to gain thy deathless praise ? "

uniformly glow with the sacred fire of liberty ; inasmuch that our public-spirited doctor well deserves to be styled the *poet of the community.* In this light we have read his Ode to the Country Gentlemen of England, with peculiar satisfaction. It is spirited, manly, and sufficiently poetical, for those to whom it is addressed ;—and as, in former times, the halls of our rural ancestors were adorned with passages from our old chronicles, so we heartily wish, that most of the stanzas of this patriotic performance were to supply the place, in our modern mansions, of race-horses, Newmarket jockies, and the trophies of the chase."

Soon after writing this poem, the author was seized with a violent sickness ; to facilitate his recovery from which, he retired, for a short time, to Goulder's Hill, the seat of Mr. Dyson ; where he had the satisfaction of hailing the arrival of a lady, whom his friend had recently married. To this agreeable circumstance he alludes in an ode, written on the occasion of his recovery. Never, in fact, was

Another writer * says, his Attic urn was
    " Fill'd from Ilyssus by the Naiad's hand."

---

* Author of the Epistle to Christopher Anstey, Esq.

any friendship more beautiful than that, subsisting
between these excellent persons !

——" While around his sylvan scene
  My DYSON led the white-wing'd hours ;
  Oft from th' Athenian academic bowers
Their sages came ; oft heard our lingering walk ;
  The Mantuan music, warbling o'er the green,—
    And oft did Tully's reverend shade,
    Though much for liberty afraid,
With us of letter'd ease or virtuous glory talk.

  But OTHER GUESTS were on their way,
    And reach'd, ere long, this favour'd grove ;
    Ev'n the celestial progeny of Jove,
Bright VENUS ! with her all-subduing son,
  Whose golden shaft most willingly obey
    The best and wisest.   As they came,
    Glad HYMEN waved his genial flame,
And sang their happy gifts, and praised their spotless throne.

  I saw, when through yon festive gate
    He led along his chosen maid,
    And to my friend with smiles presenting said :
' Receive that fairest wealth, which Heaven assign'd
    To human fortune.   Did thy lonely state
      One wish, one utmost hope, confess ?
      Behold ! she comes t' adorn and bless ;
Comes, worthy of thy heart, and equal to thy mind.' "

Though Akenside never married, it is evident
from many passages in his poems, that he was
sensibly alive to the comforts of a married state.

The loss of Parthenia occurred in early youth ;—
that of Olympia in maturer manhood :

> " Far other vows must I prefer
>   To thy indulgent power ;
> Alas ! but now I paid my tear
>   On fair OLYMPIA's virgin tomb,
>   And lo, from thence, in quest I roam
>   Of Philomela's bower."

Akenside, like many a valiant knight, had laughed
at love, when love was at a distance * ; but there
seems to have been no period of his life, in which
he was not sensible to its impressions. Parthenia and
Olympia he lost, when upon the eve of marriage
with them ; but he celebrates other ladies, and
speaks of them even with affection ; Amoret † and
Melissa ‡. To which of these he alludes in his
ode, entitled the Complaint, we are left to conjecture.

> " I know, I see
> Her merit, needs it now be shown,
>   Alas ! to me ?
> How often to myself unknown

---

* See particularly his Elegy on Love ; his Ode on Love ;
and his Ode to a Friend, unsuccessful in Love.
  † Ode x. b. ii.
  ‡ P. of I. second poem, i. v. 366.

> The graceful, gentle, virtuous maid
> Have I admired! How often said
> What joy to call a heart like hers one's own!"

The feelings of Akenside, at length, relapsed almost into indifference ; but he was always alive to the irksome destitution of comfort, which attends a protracted life of celibacy. " Let the busy, or the wise," says he, in one of his odes—

> " Let the busy or the wise
> View him with contemptuous eyes,
>   LOVE is *native to the heart.*
> *Guide its wishes as you will,*
> *Without love you'll find it still*
>   *Void in one essential part.*
>
> Me, though no peculiar fair
> Touches with a lover's care,
>   Though the pride of my desire
> Asks immortal Friendship's name,
> Asks the palm of honest fame,
>   And the old heroic lyre ;
>
> *Though the day have smoothly gone,*
> *Or to letter'd leisure known,*
>   *Or in social duty spent,*
> *Yet, at eve, my lonely breast*
> *Seeks in vain for perfect rest,*
>   *Languishes for true content."*

Akenside's respect for women peeps out every where. In one passage he calls them " chief of terrestrial nature."

——————" What sublimer pomp
Adorns the sect, where Virtue dwells on earth,
And Truth's eternal day-light shines around ;
What palm belongs to MAN's imperial front,
And WOMAN, powerful with becoming smiles,
Chief of terrestrial nature! need we now
Strive to inculcate?"

Having, in a former page, alluded to Dr. Johnson's slender appreciation of Akenside's Hymn to the Naiads, we may now insert his opinion in regard to the odes. But first in respect to the Pleasures of the Imagination.

" Mr. Murphy said, ' the Memoirs of Gray's Life set him much higher in his estimation than his poems did; for you there saw a man constantly at work in literature.' Johnson acquiesced in this, but depreciated the book ; I thought very unreasonably: for he said, ' I *forced* myself to read it, only because it was the common topic of conversation. I found it mighty dull ; and as for the style, it was fit for the second table.' Why he thought so, I was at a loss to conceive. He now gave it as his opinion, that Akenside was a superior poet both to Gray and Mason."

" I see they have published a splendid edition of Akenside's works," said Johnson, on another

K

occasion : " one bad ode may be suffered ; but a number of them makes one sick."

" Akenside's distinguished poem is on the Imagination," answered Boswell ; " but for my part, I never could admire it, so much as most people do."

" Sir," said Johnson, " I could not read it through."

" I have read it through," returned Boswell, " but I could observe no great power in it."

That Johnson,—who does not appear to have enjoyed much pleasure from the higher orders either of poetry, painting, music, or architecture,—should not be able to read the Pleasures of the Imagination through, is not much to be wondered at ;— that Boswell should have been able to recognize no great power in it is still less to be admired : since beauty and grandeur do not so much exist in the objects observed, as in the mind, observing.

The fame of Akenside, as a physician, seems now to have acquired some stability. In January, 1759, he was appointed assistant physician to St. Thomas's Hospital, and two months after principal physician ; and in the same year assistant physician to Christ's Hospital.

The next year, 1760, was distinguished by the

publication of an oration*, delivered before the College of Surgeons. The title stands thus:

" Oratio anniversaria, quam ex Harveii institutio in Theatro Collegii Regalis medicorum Londinensis, die Oct. xviii. A. MDCCLIX, habuit Marcus Akenside, M. D. Coll. Med. et Reg. Societ. Socios. Dodsley. MDCCLX."

This oration was dedicated to Dr. Reeve:—

" Viro eximio Thomæ Reeve, M. D. Præsidi dignissimo, et sociis doctissimis Collegii Regalis Medicorum Londinensis, hanc orationem illorum Jussu editam, D. D. D. Marcus Akenside†."

A copy of this work Akenside, soon after publication, sent as a present to Dr. Birch, who left it to the British Museum; in the library of which it

---

* Dodsley, 4to. One Shilling.

† " Pope has not, in his art of criticism, followed the examples of the ancients, in addressing their didactic poems to some particular person; as Hesiod to Perses; Lucretius to Memmius; Virgil to Mecænas; Horace to the Pisos; Ovid, his Fasti, to Germanicus; Oppian to Caracalla. In later times Fracastorius addressed P. Bembo; Vida the Dauphin of France. But neither Boileau in his art, nor Roscommon, nor Buckingham, in their Essays, nor Armstrong, nor AKENSIDE, have followed this practice." *Warton's Pope*, i. 270.

This error of Warton, in respect to Akenside, may be corrected by referring to page 32.

still remains, with the following MS. memorandum: *Tho. Birch, donum authoris, Martii* 20, 1760.

We may here devote a short space to Mr. JUS-TICE HARDINGE. " The first I can recollect of my own personal acquaintance with Dr. Akenside's name and muse," says he, in a letter to Mr. Nichols, " was my father's recital to me, when I was a boy at Eton school, of the Invocation to Ancient Greece, in that celebrated poem, which has been so depre-ciated by Dr. Johnson, that I fear no error of judg-ment and of taste, manifest in that criticism, can redeem the censure from heavier imputations. This inspired passage, as I think still, was recommended additionally to me by the charm of recitation, in which not even Garrick himself could be superior to Mr. Nicholas Hardinge, though he had no musical ear. But his *reading* and *repeating ear*, if I may use that phrase, was exquisite. It is very singular, but it is true, that Akenside was not a good reader of his own verse." Nor were Addison or Thomson. Virgil, on the contrary, was a very fine reader.

Mr. Justice Hardinge was a very peculiar person; and left behind him the character of " *possessing,* rather than profiting by great talents." He had a very expressive countenance, and was possessed of an admirable temper: his manners were playful, and his zeal, in favour of those he protected, is said to have been ardent and unremitting. He was nephew to the great Lord Camden; many years solicitor to Queen Charlotte; and one of the justices for the counties of Glamorgan, Radnor, and Brecon. He had a due knowledge of legal subjects: but his manner in court was, occasionally, intemperate and not sufficiently dignified. His charges, however, were greatly admired. Having been some years connected with the principality, I have frequently heard his addresses to grand-jurymen; and could not but be greatly struck with the elegance of his manner, the force of his declamation, the pliability of his deportment, and his happy facility in making classical allusions. The manner in which he delivered his charge, in respect to NAPOLEON, I shall never forget*.

* "Here, at this period of our intercourse, I should part with you, but for the times. They call upon me with an imperious voice, to animate the high spirit of the day, under your wing, if it should be the last breath of my life. That high spirit beams upon us with a golden ray of hope, that we have a deliverance at hand from the *base impostor*, as well as the *usurping tyrant*, of the continent, who would have degraded us and you, if the hand-writing on the wall had not convinced him, that slavery and life never can be reconciled in British adversaries. The most enlightened city of the civilized world, which is, in other

He was, also, a poet and a critic; of which a few specimens may not be disagreeable; since he was a friend, and, for the most part, a great admirer of

words, to name the CITY of LONDON, has countersigned, with all the sanction of its proud name, and with all the eloquence of its public spirit, our interesting appeal to the God of battles in the patriot army of Spain. Upon similar occasions I have attested your zeal for your king, and for his government, when your independent mind has approved their conduct. In honour to that independence, I dare not to recommend; but I have the courage to express a sanguine hope, that you will not part, before you have pledged congenial sentiments in your address to the king, and through him to the country, which I will gratefully and proudly forward unto his majesty's hand. We are not only enlisted in the same host, but we are enrolled in the same principle, which is British at the heart's core. It is the cause of native rights and of national independence; it is the generous hatred of a tyrant, whom nothing but the sword can meet—who violates every engagement—betrays every confidence—has polluted every thing he has touched—and is, in a human shape, the pestilence not only of the legitimate government, but of the moral world. He has been compared, by depraved or timid sycophants, to Alexander and Cæsar. The compliment is basely false: those criminal heroes, in their frenzy of ambition, had *lucid intervals* of clemency, of graceful conduct, and of social virtue:—nothing of the kind has yet escaped from him. His resemblance to our usurper, Cromwell, is a little more close; but *he* was an observer of treaties, and kept his enemies at bay by his arms —not by the tenor of his friendship,—the worst of all this tyrant's enmities.

the poet, whose life and mind I have undertaken to delineate.

" Amongst his accumulated perfidies, let me offer to your notice (in a bird's-eye view) his conduct in Spain :—

' Show me his picture ! Let me see his eyes !
That when I note another man like him,
I may avoid him.'

He was the ally of Spain—he was debtor to that power for important services—he obtained its confidence. He disunited the king from the heir-apparent, his own son—he made that son his hero—he fomented this family discord into a civil war. He then took upon himself the office of mediator, with an army at his heels, erected an intermediate government in a subordinate janissary's hand, and poured his French troops into the capital of the empire. He took the king, the heir-apparent, and the queen of Spain, with him ; he bound them hand and foot; he made the king and his heir successively abdicate their crown, when they were as free as the felon, who is confined in your gaol ; he made—oh infamy of horror ! —this queen bastardize her own legitimate son, and branded herself as a degraded prostitute ! He then quoted those very infamies against them in Spain, as proving them unworthy to return, and base to their country. Opposed in these detestable perfidies, he murdered thousands of Spaniards in cold blood ; and at last insulted that high-spirited nation with his infamous brother's election, by him, to the vacant throne !

" It is this man we are to fight ; our own deliverance and that of Europe are combined—we are to fight him locally in Spain. But I address men of good sense, equal to their high spirits. They will follow me in the sentiment, that Spain is Britain, that her cause will be felt in every inch of her coast, and of the island we inhabit."

HINTS OF THE WELSH JUDGE'S CAVALRY*.

" The Fates have doom'd without remorse
Me,—to an *old* and *wheezing* horse,—
Unless, to shift the parted blame,
I take another, which is *lame*.
A mirror of the rider's fate
Appears in his equestrian state;
It's like his *fortune*'s lingering death,—
It's lame,—it's old,—it's *out of breath*."

In another poem he fables, that he, one day, saw
his full-bottomed wig, stripped of its curls, and
swept into a corner of a passage;—upon which, he
addressed the disconsolate judicial ornament, as if
it could hear and speak :

" Emblem of all state and power,
Wing and feather of an hour !
Injured curl ! whose awful trace
Once adorn'd a Judge's face;
Once, as frightened CAMBRIA saw,
Was the Dignity of Law;
When its penthouse overhung
The Judicial Pedant's tongue;
And his venerable head
Could assume the weight of lead.

---

* He generally rode the circuit; and every now and then
took pleasure in disappointing the sheriffs, by taking a by-
road into the town, in which he was, the moment after his
arrival, to sit as Chief Judge. He is still remembered in
South Wales; particularly amongst the ladies.

Then his thunder could appal
Guilt-convicted in the Hall;
Then, with a becoming fury,
He could reprobate a jury;
Or could point his whipping wrath
At a Felon's *table-cloth* *.
Then protection he could pledge
To a *rag* upon a hedge.
Now the comb, as in despair,
Shuns the abdicated hair;
And the Maid's oblivious broom
Seems to ridicule the doom.
From the lethargy of rest
Who shall raise thy dormant crest?
April soon will pass away;
Oh, beware the *first of May* †!
Rather warn the felon crows,
Where the ripening herbage grows;
Where, though mute, thy sapient form
Still its terrors can reform;
Than degrade thee out of Court,
For the gazer's common sport;
Prohibiting all thy power
To the mob's insulting hour.

---

* " He had censured a jury for acquitting a murderer; and had sentenced a man to be whipped for stealing a table-cloth from a hedge."

† " Nothing is more shamefully familiar upon these Saturnalia to the common eye, than a judge's wig upon the face of a chimney-sweeper."

Thus when hair again was grown,
Sumson made his prowess known,
To derision's cruel mirth,
By its immolated worth."

EPITAPH ON HIMSELF.

" Here's the old Boy, whose heart was never cold,
Fond as in youth, when all the rest was old.
He without pain from house and land could part ;
But if he lost a rhyme, it broke his heart.
In vanities gay VILLIERS he surpass'd,
The new-born whims improving on the last :
Yet has this lunatic one truth impress'd—
That Fools are happy, and that life's a jest."

As a specimen of criticism we may select the following letter addressed to Mr. Mudford : —

" I am not such an enthusiast for LORD BYRON as you are, and I confess that I think WALTER SCOTT very superior to him ;—CRABBE, though a mannerist, is a particular favourite of mine. ROGERS and CAMPBELL have a thousand beauties. Lord Byron is unquestionably a gifted creature, full of genius, fancy, and poetical effect ; but he is desultory and unequal. His thoughts are often bold and original ; his expressions happy and striking ; but he is often quaint and forced in his images, at least as *I* think. But you must not kill me, if I say in my old age, I almost begin to think that *taste*, as it is called, in our judgment of the Muse, has more whim than solidity, and that our *ear* is often too imperious to be governed by rules. Nothing can be more unlike than GRAY and COWPER; yet I am enraptured of them both. I am wicked enough to think DRYDEN very superior to POPE. PRIOR and WALLER, in some of their playful graces, enchant me; but I cannot admire MASON or THOMSON."

I have paid the greater attention to Mr. Hardinge *, because he brings a charge against Akenside of political apostacy.

It is certain that Mr. Dyson forsook his party, and became a tory; but it does not appear that Akenside, whatever his friend might do, ever forsook his principles; at least, his second poem on the Pleasures of Imagination is, to the full, as remarkable for a fine glow of liberty as the first. Two or three passages may be supposed to militate against this opinion; but, I think, they will, in no respect, bear an interpretation hostile to the principles, by which Akenside seems always to have been governed. Mr. Hardinge thought otherwise. " I must not forget to mention," says he, " perhaps the most curious feature of his life. It is in the

* He died at Presteigne, April 16, 1816, in the 72d year of his age.

partial, but very awkward change, which Akenside's new politics at court made in those of the
poet.   You will find a memorable proof to this
point.   In the first edition of the work these lines
appear:

> " Wilt thou, kind Harmony, descend,
>   And join the festive train : for with thee comes
>   Majestic TRUTH ; and where TRUTH deigns to come,
>   Her sister, Liberty, will not be far."

And in the second edition,

> ————————" For with thee comes
>   * WISE ORDER ; and where ORDER deigns to come,
>   Her sister LIBERTY will not be far."

I confess, I see no derogation of principle here :
Order being the sister of Liberty as well as Truth ;
and both, as it were, the parents of that Harmony,
the poet celebrates.

In the first edition of the ode " On leaving Holland," the poet says —

> " I go where *Freedom in the streets is known,*
>   And tells a monarch on his throne,
>   *Tells him, he reigns, he lives, but by her voice."*

---

* In the MS. corrected poem the following line is introduced :
" The guide, the guardian, of their mystic rites."

In the last edition—

> " I go where *Liberty to all is known,*
> And tells a monarch on his throne,
> *He reigns not but by her preserving voice.*"

Surely there is no difference here, that can be twisted into any,—even the slightest,—variation of sentiment. Neither is there any thing of importance in the alteration, made in his Ode to the Earl of Huntingdon :—

> " But here, where freedom's equal throne,
> To all her valiant sons are known ;
> *Where all direct the sword, she wears,*
> And each the power which rules him shares."

In the subsequent editions (third line),

> " *Where all are conscious of her cares.*"

No one can have a greater contempt for the administration of Lord Bute than I have; but Mr. Dyson might have been a supporter of that minister, and yet Akenside remain innocent of the change. That courtly acquaintance might have an influence on the mind of a physician, desirous of practice, is not to be wondered at; but that he ever became as zealous a partisan of the Tories, as he had been of the Whigs, is not only not to be credited, but is an assertion, that bears within itself the balance of a contradiction.   For, had he been as zealous a lover of too extended an authority, as he had previously been of Liberty and a due administration of the laws, he would, like many,—I had almost said most,—of his poetical brethren, have left something better behind him, wherewith to mark the change, than some of the finest sentiments, that human language will admit of.   I have, I say, a strong dislike to the memory of the BUTE and NORTH administrations; but I still think, that a physician might be so prudent as not to offend a party, which had advanced him; and yet remain a decided enemy to the foes of his country, whether from within or from without.

Even so late as 1770, the year in which he died, Akenside wrote lines; than which nothing can breathe a purer spirit, or be indicative of a more exalted imagination.

> ——————————— " Nor shall e'er
> The graver tasks of manhood, or th' advice
> Of vulgar wisdom move me to disclaim
> Those studies, which possess'd me in the dawn
> Of life, and fix'd the colour of my mind,
> For every future year."
>
> *P. I. Second Poem,* iv. v. 46.

In his third book, too,—finished long after the

period of which we have been lately speaking, with what contempt and ridicule does he visit——

———————————— " The abject soul,
Who, blushing, half resigns the candid praise
Of temperance and honour ; half disowns
A freeman's hatred of tyrannic pride,
And hears, with sickly smiles, the venal mouth,
With foulest licence, mock the patriot's name＊."
P. I. Second Poem, l. 222.

Indeed, that his love of true liberty had become, in no degree, impaired by political associations, is not only evident from the passages above quoted, but from the circumstance of the whole episode of Solon having been written with no other design, than that of showing the influence, which poetry has in duly enforcing the cause and interests of freedom.

In the second poem there is an alteration, strikingly confirmative of the preceding observations : —previous to exhibiting which, however, I shall state an

---

＊ His contempt of flattery, when addressed to tyrants, is amply shown in his appreciation of Horace :

" Whose verse adorn'd a tyrant's crimes ;
Who saw majestic Rome betray'd,
And lent the imperial ruffian aid."

alteration, which occurs in the MS. corrected copy
of the first.

ORIGINAL.

——————————— " Nor be my thoughts
Presumptuous counted, if amid the calm,
That soothes this vernal evening into smiles,
I steal, impatient, from the sordid haunts
Of STRIFE and low AMBITION, to attend
Thy sacred presence in the sylvan shade,
By their malignant footsteps ne'er profaned."

MS. CORRECTION.

" If I from SUPERSTITION's gloomy haunts
Impatient steal, and from th' unseemly rites
Of barbarous DOMINATION, to attend
With hymns thy presence in the lonely shades,
By their malignant footsteps unprofaned."

In the SECOND Poem :

" If I, from vulgar superstition's walk,
Impatient, steal, and from th' unseemly rites
Of splendid ADULATION, to attend
With hymns," &c.

These alterations are very curious. First, he
desires to steal from strife and low ambition ; then
from the gloomy haunts of superstition and domination ; lastly, not only from the haunts of ambition,
but the unseemly rites of splendid adulation. The

first denotes the period of youth, when life was opening upon him in the midst of low-minded persons; the next, when he had entered the high career of existence, and was, no doubt, taunted with the thoughts he bore to the exquisite advantages of universal toleration; the last when he had entered the precincts of a court, and saw flattery assume a form, that could not be otherwise than revolting to an elegant and noble mind.

In 1763, Akenside communicated the following account of a blow and its effects upon the heart, to the Royal Society, where it was read Dec. 22, and soon after published in the Philosophical Transactions.

" On the 11th of September, 1762, Richard Bennet, a lad about fourteen years of age, was brought to a consultation of the physicians and surgeons of St. Thomas's hospital. His disorder was a palpitation of the heart ; so very violent to the touch, that we all concluded it to be an aneurism, and without remedy. He had a frequent cough. His pulse was quick, weak, and uneven; but not properly intermitting. It was apparent that nothing could be done, farther than by letting blood in small quantities, and by the use of emollient pectoral medicines, to lessen, now and then, however inconsiderably, the extreme danger to which he was continually subject.   He was taken into the hospital that same day, being Saturday; and treated according to what had been agreed upon.   But on the Tuesday morning following he died, without any previous alarm or alteration.

" The origin of his complaint was a blow, which he had received six months before, from the master whom he served, as a waiter in a public-house.   The master owned, that he had pushed him slightly on the left side with his hand.   The boy informed us, that he himself was then carrying a plate under his arm; and that the blow or push from his master drove the edge of the plate forcibly between two of his ribs.   He was immediately very ill from the hurt; sick, and in great pain. His mother, also, informed us, that she thought the palpitation was more violent about a fortnight after the accident, than when we examined him.   The day after the blow, they took eight ounces of blood from his arm; about three weeks after that they again opened a vein, but got not much from it; and three weeks from thence, they let him blood the last time to the amount of eight ounces.   He began to have a cough soon after the hurt, with frequent spittings of blood in very large quantities; and had nocturnal sweats almost the whole six months, during which he survived the blow. About four months after it, there came over the umbilical region of the abdomen, a livid appearance like a mortification: but it went off gradually, and at length vanished.   He had nothing particular in his habit of body or state of health; save that, about a year before this accident, he had been crippled with the rheumatism.   He was, when we saw him, a good deal reduced; but had not a hectic nor a consumptive look.

" On the day of his death Mr. Cowell opened him; when, to our great surprise, we found no aneurism, nor the least extravasation of the blood, either from the cavities of the heart, or the large vessels. But on the left ventricle of the heart, near its apex, there was a livid spot, almost as large as a half-crown piece, bruised and jelly-like; the part underneath being mortified quite to the cavity of the ventricle. From thence upward, toward the auricle, there went several livid specks and traces of inflammation, tending in like manner to gangrene. The heart did also, through its whole surface, adhere very closely to the pericardium; and the whole outer surface of the pericardium as closely to the lungs. The other viscera were quite sound.

" So that the mischief here was properly a contusion of the heart; the edge of the plate having struck it, probably at the instant of its greatest diastole. This produced an inflammation on its surface, followed by a gangrene, and terminating in that double adhesion: by which the whole heart was fast tied up; till, on this account, as well as by reason of the mortification, it was no longer able to circulate the blood."

In 1764, Akenside published the most important of his medical works; viz. *De Dysenteria Commentarius*. On this work the medical fame of

* De Dysenteria Commentarius. Auctore Marco Akenside, Coll. Med. Londin. Socio. Reg. Societ. Sodali, et Magnæ

Akenside principally rests. The dysentery seems to have been very little understood before his time; and he attributes the causes to nearly the same as those of the rheumatism, between which, he insists, there is a great affinity. Hence he calls the bloody flux a rheumatism of the intestines*; and he recommends, as a cure, the bleeding of persons of a full habit; and certain portions of ipecacuanha. To cure the diarrhœa, which so frequently succeeds the flux, he recommends particularly one ounce of fresh mutton suet, melted in a pint of boiling milk.

The causes of the action of ipecacuanha on the subjects of this distemper, he resolves into its aperient power, and its faculty of relaxing the coats of the intestines, and thence abating the violence of

Britanniæ Reginæ Medico. Londini: apud R. et I. Dodsley. MDCCLXIV.

Table of Contents :

* " Denique hanc morborum similitudinem toties jam observavi et perspexi, ut Dysenteriam jamdudum pro Rheumatismo intestinorum habeam—nos vero, id vocabulum a doloribus artuum et musculorum ad intestina transferendo, similem plane utriusque morbi causam et materiam esse contendimus."

the tenesmus. In short, he supposes it to possess a kind of anodyne and antispasmodic virtue, which no other opiate possesses in this distemper; which he, contrary to the opinions of Sydenham *, and Boerhaave, whom he styles—" ingeniossimus et candidissimus," and Mead †, thinks ought seldom to be classed among acute diseases ‡.

The latinity of this work is singularly pure and elegant; and to advance a knowledge of its contents, Dr. Ryan undertook to translate it; but this version being faulty in many respects, Mr. Motteux attempted it: neither versions, however, are remarkable for style, or even for a close adherence to the author's text.

In 1766, Akenside published his ode to THOMAS EDWARDS, ESQ. It was printed in folio, published

* Vid. Observat. de Morb. Acut., sect. i. c. 2, sect. iv. c. 3.

† Vid. Monita et Præcept. Med. c. vii. sect. 1.

‡ The use of ipecacuanha in this disorder appears to have been some time known on the Continent; for we read in the life of Helvetius, p. vi., that Adrian, grandfather to Helvetius, gained great reputation in Holland, by discovering a cure for the dysentery by the exhibition of ipecacuanha. Vid. also *Piso, de Indiæ utriusque re Naturali et Medica.* " Drachmæ duæ radicis ipecacuanha in ℥iiij liquoris appropriati coctæ, vel per noctem maceratæ, cujus infusum cum vel sine oxymelis ℥j exhibetur."—Lib. ii. c. ix. The Amsterdam edition, which is by far the best, has it c. xi.

by Dodsley, and sold for sixpence.   This ode had
been written as early as 1751 ; and it has created
surprise, that he should have so long withheld
the publication.   Doubtless, his anger against
Dr. Warburton had long subsided ; but Warburton, now become Bishop of Gloucester, inflamed
it again by publishing a new edition of the Divine
Legation of Moses, with the obnoxious postscript
he had before appended to his preface ; and that,
too, without any reference to the arguments, which
had been adduced on the other side,—a practice not
unusual with the learned bishop, who seems to have
thought, on most occasions, that an attack upon
him, even when in self-defence, was as great a crime
as treason against the state.   " And yet, who is
Dr. Warburton ?" inquired Mr. Edwards, " what
is his birth, and whence his privilege ? that the
reputations of men, both living and dead, of men
in birth, character, station, in every instance of true
worthiness, much his superiors, must lie at the
mercy of his petulant satire, to be hacked and
mangled, as his ill-mannered spleen shall prompt
him ; while it shall be unlawful for any body, under
penalty of degradation, to laugh at the unscholarlike
blunders, the crude and far-fetched conceits, the
illiberal and indecent reflections, which he has en-

deavoured, with so much self-sufficiency and arrogance, to put off upon the world, as a standard of true criticism *."

MR. EDWARDS was descended from a family, which had, for many years, been settled at Pitzhanger, in the county of Middlesex. He was educated at Eton; whence he removed to King's College, Cambridge; but after graduating there some time, he determined, since his fortune was limited, neither to study the law, divinity, nor physic; but to enter the army. He afterwards altered his plan, quitted the military life, entered himself at Lincoln's Inn, and, after the usual terms, was called to the bar.

At this period Akenside became acquainted with him; and their acquaintance soon ripened into esteem, and thence into friendship. Mr. Edwards, like his associate, was an accomplished scholar. His manners were mild and bland, and his disposition affectionate to the last degree. He was the last of his family; and as the sonnet, he wrote on seeing a family picture, which brought to his recollection the melancholy circumstance of his having lost four brothers, and four sisters, is remarkable for an elegant and pathetic simplicity, I shall quote it.

* Canons of Criticism. Pref. 7. 3d ed. 1750.

ON A FAMILY PICTURE.

" When pensive on that portraiture I gaze,
　　Where my four BROTHERS round about me stand
　　And four fair SISTERS smile with graces bland,
　The goodlier monument of happier days;
　And think, how soon insatiate Death, who preys
　　On all, has cropp'd the rest with ruthless hand,
　　While only I survive of all that band,
　Which one chaste bed did to my father raise;
　　It seems that like a column left alone,
　The tottering remnant of some splendid fane,
　　'Scaped from the fury of the barb'rous Gaul,
　　And wasting time, which has the rest o'erthrown,
　Amidst our house's ruin I remain,
　　Single, unprop'd, and nodding to my fall."

Besides this sonnet, Mr. Edwards wrote many
others; several of which are preserved in Dodsley's,
Pearch's, and Nichols' collections. But the work,
which raised him to a rank with men of letters,
was his CANONS of CRITICISM, written in direct
hostility to Warburton, on his having published
an edition of Shakspeare;—an edition which laid
the reverend editor but too justly open to critical
retaliation.

Between Dr. Warburton and Mr. Edwards there
had, for some time, existed a very strong mutual
dislike; the cause of which is thus stated in the

Gentleman's Magazine *. " Being at Bath, some time after he went into the army, Mr. Edwards, not long after the marriage of Warburton with Mr. Allen's † niece, was introduced *en famille*. The conversation was, not unfrequently, turning on literary subjects, and Warburton generally took the opportunity of showing his superiority in Greek ; not having the least idea, that an officer in the army understood any thing of that language ;— till, one day, being accidentally in the library, Mr. Edwards took down a Greek author, and explained a passage in it in a manner, that Warburton did not approve. This occasioned no small

* Vol. liii. p. 288.

† Mr. Allen was a man of plain good sense, and the most benevolent temper. He rose to great consideration by farming the cross-posts; which he put into the admirable order, in which we now find them ; very much to the public advantage, as well as his own. He was of that generous disposition, that his mind enlarged with his fortune ; and the wealth, he so honourably acquired, he spent in a splendid hospitality, and the most extensive charities. His house, in so public a scene, as that of Bath, was open to all men of rank and worth, and especially to men of distinguished parts and learning ; whom he honoured and encouraged ; and whose respective merits he was enabled to appreciate by a natural discernment and superior good sense, rather than any acquired use and knowledge of letters. His domestic virtues were beyond all praise.—*Hurd's Life of Warburton, p. 45.*

contest; and Mr. Edwards (who had now discovered to Warburton, how he came by his knowledge) endeavoured to convince him, that he did
not understand the original language; and hinted
that his knowledge arose from French translations.
Warburton was highly irritated; an incurable
breach took place; and this trifling altercation (after
Mr. Edwards had quitted the army, and was entered of Lincoln's Inn) produced the Canons of
Criticism."

This work is not now often referred to; the
occasion, for which it was written, having passed
away; but as its table of contents exhibits no slight
degree of that species of humour, for which Swift
has been so greatly celebrated, I shall give an abstract of it in a note *.

* A professed critic has a right to declare, that his author
wrote whatever he ought to have written, with as much de-
termination, as if he had been at his elbow[1]; that he has a
right to alter any passage he does not understand[2]; and that
these alterations he may make, in spite of the exactness of the
measure[3].

Where he does not like an expression, and cannot mend
it, he may abuse his author for it[4]; or he may condemn it as
an idle interpolation[5]. As every author is to be corrected into
all possible perfection[6]; and of that perfection the critic is

---

[1] Canons, p. 1.   [2] p. 5.   [3] p. 25.   [4] p. 30.   [5] p. 32.   [6] p. 34.

Dr. Warton says of these Canons, " all impartial critics allow, that they remain unrefuted and unanswerable."

the sole judge, it follows, as a matter of course, that he may alter any word or phrase, which does not want amendment, or which will do, provided he can think of any thing, which he imagines will do better. He may, also, find out obsolete words, or coin new ones, and put them in the place of such as he does not like, or does not understand [1].

He may prove a reading, or support an explanation by any sort of reading, good or bad, provided he likes it [2]; he may interpret his author, so as to make him mean directly contrary to what he says [3]; he is under no necessity of allowing any poetical licences, which he does not understand [4]; and he may make any amendments, however foolish; and give any explanations, whether those explanations are wanted or not, provided he can, by those amendments or explanations, enhance the value of his critical skill [5].

He may discover any immoral meaning in his author, where there does not appear to be any hint of the kind [6]: he is under no obligation himself to attend to such trivial matters as orthography or pointing; but he may ridicule, as much as he pleases, such trivial errors in others [7]. Yet, when he pleases to condescend to such matters, he may value himself upon it; and not only restore lost puns, but point out such quaintnesses, where, perhaps, the author never thought of them [8]. He may explain a difficult passage by words, absolutely unintelligible [9]; and he may contradict himself for

---

[1] Canons, p. 42.   [2] p. 58.   [3] p. 83.   [4] p. 94.   [5] p. 96.
[6] p. 98.   [7] p. 101.   [8] p. 104.   [9] 108.

Akenside had not forgotten the contemptuous manner in which his theory, in respect to the subject of ridicule, had been treated by Warburton. The Canons of Criticism, therefore, united him

the sake of showing his critical skill on both sides [1]; and he should take care to be provided, beforehand, with a good number of pedantic and abusive expressions, to throw about upon proper occasions [2].

He may explain his author, or any former editor of him, by supplying such words, or pieces of words, or marks, as he may think fit for that purpose [3]; and he may use the very same reasons for confirming his own observations, which he has disallowed in his adversary [4].

As the design of writing notes is not so much to explain the author's meaning, as to display the critic's knowledge [5]; it may be proper, to show his universal learning, that he minutely point out from whence every metaphor and allusion is taken. It will be, also, especially if he be a married man, proper, in order to show the greatness of his wit, to take every opportunity of sneering at the fair sex [6]:—he may misquote himself, or any body else, in order to make an occasion of writing notes, when he cannot otherwise find one [7]; and, lest he may not furnish a proper quota to his bookseller, he may write notes out of nothing [8]; and lastly [9], he may dispense with truth at all times, and in any manner agreeable to himself, provided, by these violations, he can give the world a higher opinion, than it would otherwise entertain, that he is a man of great parts.

---

[*] Canons, p. 110.   [2] p. 112.   [3] p. 114.   [4] p. 118.   [5] p. 119.   [6] p. 128.   [7] p. 132.   [8] p. 134.   [9] p. 141.

more intimately with Mr. Edwards. For as Warburton's attack upon his philosophy had produced
some effects, little favourable to his fame as a poet,
he feared it might also, perhaps, prove, in some
degree, injurious to him as a physician.

Why he delayed the publication of his ode for
so long a period as fifteen years, viz. from 1751 to
1766, does not appear; but when he did publish it,
it produced effects, very important for a time, to
the fame of a critic, who had revelled in the almost
unlimited authority, which he took pleasure in
establishing within the empire of criticism. For,
in a note, appended to this ode, Akenside roundly
charged the right reverend critic with having zeal-
ously cultivated the friendship of Theobald and
Concanen with the rest of the tribe, who confe-
derated against Pope. In proof of which, he produced a letter, which had been written by Warburton in 1726. " This letter," says Akenside,
" was found in the year 1750, by Dr. Gavin Knight,
first librarian to the British Museum, in fitting up
a house, which he had taken in Crane-court, Fleet-
street. The house had, for a long time before, been
let in lodgings, and in all probability, Concanen had
lodged there. The original letter has been many
years in my possession, and is here most exactly

copied, with its several little peculiarities in grammar, spelling, and punctuation.—*April* 30, 1766. *M. A.*"

Letter from Mr. W. Warburton to Mr. M. Concanen.

" **Dear Sir,**

" Having had no more regard for those papers, which I spoke of and promised to Mr. Theobald, than just what they deserved, I in vain sought for them through a number of loose papers that had the same kind of abortive birth. I used to make it one good part of my amusement in reading the English poets, those of them I mean whose view flows regularly and constantly, as well as clearly, to trace them to their sources ; and observe what oar, as well as what slime and gravel they brought down with them. Dryden I observe borrows for want of leasure, and Pope for want of Genius ; Milton out of pride, and Addison out of modesty. And now I speak of this latter, that you and Mr. Theobald may see of what kind those Idle collections are, and likewise to give you my notion of what we may safely pronounce an Imitation, for it is not I presume the same train of Ideas, that follow in the same description of an Ancient and a modern, where nature autorize us to pronounce the latter an Imitation, for the most judicious of all poets, Terence, has observed of his own science, ' *Nihil est dictum, quod non sit dictum prius :*' for these reasons I say I give myselfe the pleasure of setting down some imitations I observed in the Cato of Addison.

'ADDISON.

'A day, an hour of virtuous liberty
Is worth a whole eternity in bondage.'

Act II. Sc. 1.

' TULLY.

' *Quod si immortalitas consequeretur præsentis periculi fugam, tamen eo magis ea fugienda esse videretur, quo diuturnior esset servitus.*'—PHILIPP. OR. 10.

'ADDISON.

' Bid him disband his legions,
   Restore the commonwealth to liberty,
   Submit his actions to the public censure,
   And stand the judgement of a Roman Senate;
   Bid him do this, and Cato is his friend.'

' TULLY.

' *Pacem vult? arma deponat, roget, deprecetur. Neminem equiorem reperiet quam me.*'—PHILIPP. 5.

'ADDISON.

————————' But what is life ?
'Tis not to stalk about and draw fresh air
From time to time——
'Tis to be free.   When liberty is gone,
Life grows insipid and has lost its relish.'

Sc. 3.

' TULLY.

' *Non enim in spiritu vita est: sed ea nulla est omnino servienti.*'—PHILIPP. 10.

' ADDISON.

' Remember. O my friends, the laws, the rights,
The generous plan of power deliver'd down
From age to age by your renowned forefathers.
O never let it perish in your hands.'

Act III. Sc. 5.

' TULLY.

————' *Hanc (libertatem scilt) retirete, quæso, Quirites,
quam vobis, tanquam hereditatem, majores nostri reliquerunt.'*
PHILIPP. 4.

' ADDISON.

' The mistress of the world, the seat of empire,
The nurse of heroes, the Delight of Gods.'

' TULLY.

' *Roma domus virtutis, imperii dignitatis, domicilium
gloriæ, lux orbis terrarum.'*——DE ORATORE.

"The first half of the 5 Sc., 3 Act, is nothing but
a transcript from the 9 book of Lucan between the
300 and the 700 line. You see by this specimen
the exactness of Mr. Addison's judgement who wanting
sentiments worthy the Roman consul sought for them
in Tully and Lucan. When he would give his subject
those terrible graces which Dion. Halicar. complains he
could find no where but in Homer, he takes the assistance of our Shakespear, who in his *Julius Cæsar* has
painted the conspirators with a pomp and terrour, that
perfectly astonishes. Hear our British Homer:

'Between the acting of a dreadful thing,
And the first motion, all the Int'rim is
Like a phantasma, or a hideous dream ;
The Genius and the mortal Instruments
Are then in *council,* and the state of man,
Like to a little kingdom, suffers then
The nature of an insurrection.'

Mr. Addison has thus imitated it :——

'O think what anxious moments pass between
The birth of plots, and their last fatal periods !
O 'tis a dreadful interval of time,
Fill'd up with horror all, and big with death !'

"I have two things to observe on this imitation :——
I. The decorum this master of propriety has observed.
In the Conspiracy of Shakespear's description, the fortunes of Cæsar and the Roman Empire were concerned ;
and the magnificent circumstances of

'The Genius and the mortal Instruments
Are then in council,'

is exactly proportioned to the dignity of the subject.
But this would have been too great an apparatus to the
desertion of Syphax and the rape of Sempronius, and
therefore Mr. Addison omits it. II. The other thing
more worth our notice is, that Mr. A. was so greatly
moved and affected with the pomp of Shakespear's description, that *instead of copying his Author's sentiments,*
he has before he was aware given us only the marks of
his own impressions on the reading him. For,

M

‘ O ’tis a dreadful interval of time,
Fill’d up with horror all, and big with death !’

are but the affections raised by such lively images as
these—

——————— ‘ all the Int’rim is
Like a phantasma or a hideous dream ;’

and,

——————— ‘ the state of man,
Like to a little kingdom, suffers then
The nature of an insurrection.’

“ Again, when Mr. Addison would paint the softer
passions, he has recourse to Lee, who certainly had a
peculiar genius that way : thus, his Juba,

‘ True she is fair—O how divinely fair !’

coldly imitates Lee in his Alex. :

“ Then he would talk :—good gods, how he would talk !”

I pronounce the more boldly of this, because Mr. A.
in his 39 Spec. expresses his admiration of it. My
paper fails me, or I should now offer to Mr. Theobald
an objection against Shakespear’s acquaintance with the
ancients. As it appears to me of great weight, and as it
is necessary he should be prepared to obviate all that
occur on that head. But some other opportunity will
present itselfe. You may now, sʳ, justly complain of
my ill manners in deferring till now, what shou’d have
been first of all acknowledged due to you, which is my

thanks for all your favours when in town, particularly for introducing me to the knowledge of those worthy and ingenious gentlemen that made up our last night's conversation. I am, sir, with all esteem your most obliged friend and humble servant,

" W. WARBURTON.

" *Newarke, Jan. 2. 1726.*

" For
>   *Mr. M. Concanen at*
>   *Mr. Woodward's at the*
>   *half moon in ffleetstreet*
>   *London.*"

It is unnecessary to enter much into the history of this subject. Concanen, to whom Warburton thus familiarly writes, was author of a multitude of scurrilities in the London journals; in which he accused Pope of passing off Broome's verses, as well as those of the Duke of Buckingham, for his own *; and, having thrown out some abuse against Lord Bolingbroke, became acquainted with Sir Wm. Yonge; and having written for Sir Robert Walpole, he was made Attorney-General of Jamaica.

Thus promoted, he married an opulent widow; returned to London in 1748, (whether upon his

---

* Warburton.

M 2

own resignation, or from having been turned out by Governor Trelawney is not decided); and died, very rich, of a consumption in 1749.   He is thus stigmatized in the Dunciad *—

> " True to the bottom, see Concanen creep,
>   A cold, long-winded native of the deep :
>   If perseverance gain the diver's prize,
>   Not everlasting Blackmore this denies.
>   No noise, no stir, no motion canst thou make ;
>   Th' unconscious stream sleeps o'er thee like a lake."

The Ode to Mr. Edwards †, to illustrate which the preceding very remarkable letter has been introduced, was written in derision of Warburton's edition of Pope: and soon after its publication, the two following curious letters appeared in the Public Advertiser.

" *To the Printer of the Public Advertiser.*

" Sir,

     " Amidst that torrent of abuse, which is daily pouring out on the most illustrious characters of the age, the learned Bishop of G——— could not fail to come

---

* Book II. 299.

† Mr. Edwards spent the latter part of his life at Turrick ; died when on a visit to his friend, Mr. Richardson, at Parson's Green, unmarried ; and was buried at Ellesborough in Buckinghamshire.—*Nichols.*

in for his share.   To omit numberless other instances, a thing, called ' An Ode to J. Edwards, Esq.' (him of the Dunciad), is just published, and retailed with much industry, in the public prints.   The writer, it seems, is Dr. AKENSIDE ; and the date, as we are told in the title page, 1751.

" What provocation the Doctor then had for this ingenious piece of revenge, every body understands ; but what determined him to make it public at this time may require to be explained.   The secret, I suppose, is no more than this :—The bishop has, just now, given a new edition of the first volume of his Divine Legation ; and has thought fit to reprint the *Censure,* he had before made on a certain note of this poet—that very *Censure,* which had occasioned the ingenious Ode of 1751. *Hinc illæ lachrymæ.*   But what ! the reader will say, this censure is of a critical and controversial kind : it shows Dr. Akenside to be an ill-reasoner, and how is this charge evaded by the Doctor's attempt to show the Bishop to be an ill man ?   Certainly, not at all : but it was something to blacken whom he could not refute.

" In the mean time, the triumphant superiority of the Bishop's pen is very conspicuous.   But who, that could have answered the *Writer,* would have had the meanness to attack the *Man ?*

" But what, after all, is this attack ?   Why, the Bishop, it seems, thought favourably of a dunce, then his acquaintance, and entertained some unfavourable sentiments of a wit, afterwards his friend.   And what is there in all this (admitting the fact to be as related), which can be thought to lessen the character of

the learned Prelate ?   What great man has *never* made
an acquaintance with a little one ?   Or, what wise man
has *never* been misled by Prejudice ?   I am not in the
secret of the Bishop's History ; but I could tell the
Doctor of many dull men, whom this generous Prelate
has had the condescension to treat with more civility,
than they deserved ; and if he has had his prejudices
against some ingenious men, I could tell him how
frankly, upon better information, they have been given
up.   The truth is, these petty cavils give no shock to a
great character, which ever sustains itself by its own
proper merits, and is sure to have justice done it, when
the offensive splendour of those merits is withdrawn.
For, as his great friend (to whom, and to dulness, the
Bishop has long since atoned for any injustice, he might
formerly have done to either), said divinely well,

> ' Direct we feel their beam intensely beat ;
> These suns of glory please not till they set.'

            " I am, Sir,
                    " Your humble servant,
                            " J. L.

  " *May 6, 1766.*"

        " *To the Printer of the Public Advertiser.*

  " SIR,
            " OBSERVING in your paper of May 10 some
strictures upon an Ode to T. Edwards, Esq., ascribed
to Dr. Akenside, it brought to my mind another piece
of poetry, entitled *The Pleasures of Imagination,* pub-

lished about twenty years ago, and ascribed to the same author; in which are the following lines:

> ' Others of graver mien, behold; adorn'd
> With holy ensigns, how sublime they move,
> And, bending oft their sanctimonious eyes,
> Take homage of the simple-minded throng,
> Ambassadors of heaven.'

This passage, it seems, gave offence to the learned writer, who is supposed to be the subject of the little piece of satire inscribed to Mr. Edwards, above-mentioned; and who, in a preface to some *Remarks on several occasional Reflections*, published in 1744, calls these lines ' an insult on the whole body of the Christian clergy;' and comments upon them thus :—

" ' And well do they (the clergy) deserve this *moral ridicule*, supposing them to be drawn *like :* for, if I understand any thing of colouring, the features are pride, hypocrisy, fraud, and imposture. I call it an insult on the whole body of the clergy, because I know of no part of them, who hold that the ministry of the Gospel (or, as *St. Paul* calls it, of *Reconciliation*), was given them by the religion of CHRIST, but hold likewise' with the same apostle (who speaks of himself here as a simple minister of the Gospel), that they are *ambassadors* for CHRIST.'

" Whether Dr. Akenside intended the description, contained in these lines, for the whole body of the Christian clergy, must be left to his own conscience; for I do not know, that he ever explained himself farther upon the subject. If he included the whole body of the clergy in the description, it is, doubtless, an insult upon them all ; but, in my opinion, there is no occasion to understand the words in that extent. The lines contain a description of a sort of *personal demeanour*, which, Dr. Akenside must have known, is not common to ALL the clergy. And it is obvious enough, that it cost the learned commentator some pains to accommodate the poetry with *his* interpretation. But let us now attend to another piece of poetry.

" In the year 1743 (the year immediately preceding the publication of this Reproof to Dr. Akenside) came out a pompous edition of the *Dunciad* in 4to, enriched with some *additional* remarks as we are informed in an advertisement, placed immediately after the title leaf, and signed with the initials W. W. The world (with what justice I pretend not to say) ascribed the *additional* Remarks to the same learned hand, who commented, as above, upon the passage, cited from Dr. Akenside's poem.

" In this edition of the Dunciad, we meet with the following lines, at page 113.

' He ceas'd, and spread the robe; the crowd confess
The rev'rend Flamen in his lengthen'd dress.
Around him wide a sable army stand,
A low-born, cell-bred, selfish, servile band,
Prompt or to guard or stab, to saint or damn,
Heav'n's Swiss, who fight for any God or man.'

" On these we have the following *additional* remark :
' It is to be hoped, that the satire in these lines will be

understood in the confined sense, in which the author meant it, of *such only of the clergy,* who, though solemnly engaged in the service of religion, dedicate themselves to servile and corrupt ends, to that of ministers or factions : and, though educated under an entire ignorance of the world, aspire to interfere in the government of it, and consequently to disturb and disorder it,' &c.

" How the remarker could hope this, as there is no more (if so much), in these lines, than in those of Dr. Akenside, to limit to a certain, *such of the clergy only,* I cannot perceive. He says, *the author meant it so.* If he did, he expressed his meaning very awkwardly; for the comment puts a restriction upon the text, which the words can, by no artifice, be brought to admit of; as the poet, beyond all shadow of a doubt, intended to characterize the religious as well as the political achievements of these *heavenly Swiss.* In my opinion, Pope has given his description more of the air of an universal character, than the lines of Dr. Akenside exhibit ; and if I may have leave to go the round about way, after Dr. Akenside's commentator, I think I can prove it. For example ; the *Swiss of Heaven* must be soldiers in the pay of Heaven; and what clergyman, who professes to be a soldier of JESUS CHRIST, *in view of the prize of his high calling, a crown of righteousness,* but will acknowledge himself one of *Heaven's Swiss:* whereas, if I am rightly informed, the drudges of the ministry are looked upon, even by the order itself, rather to be the ambassadors of their superiors in office, than ambassadors immediately deputed by commissions from Heaven;

at least, till they rise to stations, in which the character may be supported with suitable dignity.

*   *   *   *   *   *

" I have not the pleasure to have the least personal knowledge of Dr. AKENSIDE; but from his general character must conclude, that he has no objection to connexions of esteem and friendship with ingenious and liberal-minded men among the English clergy, any more than with scholars and gentlemen of other professions: and as *some* of these would certainly not come under the description given in those lines of his, above cited; it cannot be fairly supposed, he meant them for a satire upon the whole order, whatever his own religious sentiments might be.

" Mr. Pope had quite other reasons for being disgusted with the English established clergy of his own times. He was a Roman Catholic; they were Protestants, whose principles and duty to the government were inducements to them to exercise their attention and vigilance against the superstition and disloyalty of the members of the church of Rome, to the political as well as religious doctrines of which Mr. Pope betrays, in some of his writings, a very strong attachment, notwithstanding his affected neutrality on particular occasions. It is, therefore, highly probable, that *his* little piece of satire was intended to comprehend the whole body of the English clergy; and this the rather, as, when the verses were first penned, it is likely, he had no experience, that there was so remarkable an exception to the general character, he had given of the clergy, as he afterwards found in the course of his friendship with that steady, pious, simple-minded, consistent, humble, and peaceable divine, to whom he consigned the sole privilege of commenting upon his works: for as to his connexions with Atterbury and Swift, he must be very sensible, with all his seeming friendship for them, that there was nothing in *their* characters, that would require to have the censure limited either with respect to them, or some others of the same stamp, with whom he might happen to have some accidental acquaintance.

"I find, indeed, that it is a problem with some critics, whom I have consulted on the present occasion, whether if the connexion with *Theobald, Concanen,* &c. had lasted a little longer, and if, during that connexion, and an estrangement from Mr. Pope, it had fallen within the province of the Remarker on Dr. Akenside's poem, to *benotify* the Dunciad; it is, I say, a question of some people, whether, in that case, Mr. Pope would not have been chastised with as much severity as Dr. Akenside was, the year following, for *insulting the whole body of the Christian Clergy.*

"I am, Sir,

"Your humble servant,

"CONTRASTER."

———————

The opinions of Akenside were in strict accordance with Whig principles. Hence arose the admiration of Mr. HOLLIS. That gentleman, however, extended his partialities so much farther than Akenside, that he was actually, in principle, a Republican.

Hence, when he purchased a bed, in 1761, which had once belonged to Milton, and in which that great poet died, he presented it to " that modern poet, whom he thought, not only in political sentiments but in poetical genius, most resembled him." The bed was accompanied with the following note:

" An English gentleman is desirous of having " the honour to present a bed, which once belonged " to JOHN MILTON, and on which he died ; and if " DR. AKENSIDE, believing himself obliged, and " having slept on that bed, should prompt him to " write an ode to the memory of John Milton, and " the assertor of British liberty, that gentleman " would think himself abundantly recompensed."

Akenside is said to have received the present with satisfaction ; but whether he wrote an ode, as requested, does not appear. It is most probable, that he did write one ; but that he could not please himself in the execution.

Akenside was never a Republican ;—he was an ardent supporter of the principles, which seated King William on the throne of this country. Mr. Dyson's opinions were the same ; but, on the accession of George the Third, and the elevation of Lord Bute, he had relaxed the severity of his declarations ; and having been admitted into the administration, had sufficient influence to get his friend appointed Physician to the Queen, who was, every day, expected to land.

Soon after Akenside's return from Holland, he had been admitted, by *mandamus*, to the same degree at Cambridge, that he had taken at Leyden. When that university sent up a congratulatory address to the King and Queen, on their marriage, therefore, he accompanied the deputation :—but, having no band, he wrote to Dr. Birch to lend him one.

" Dr. Akenside presents his compliments to Dr.
" Birch, and begs the favour, that he would lend
" him a band, in order that he may attend the
" Cambridge Address to-morrow.

" *Craven-street,*
" *Sept.* 13, 1761."

As there are only a few letters (or notes) of Akenside known to be in existence, except some to Mr. Dyson, which will be mentioned in a subsequent page, perhaps I may be excused for introducing two of them in this place. Their subjects are not very important ; but having been written by so eminent a person,—unimportant as they are in other respects, they cannot be considered in any other light than as interesting curiosities.

" DEAR SIR,

" I return you many thanks for the pleasure,
" which I have had in reading these books.

" I see, this instant, in the Public Advertiser,
" that Dr. Warburton is made King's Chaplain,
" and enters into waiting immediately.   Can you
" tell me, whether this is true?   If there be any
" hazard of finding him at Kensington, I shall not
" choose to go thither to-day.

" I am your affectionate

" humble servant,

" M. AKENSIDE.

" *Bloomsbury-square,*
" *Saturday morn. Sept.* 28.

" To the Rev. Dr. Birch,
" in Norfolk-street."

" Dr. Akenside presents his compliments to Dr.
" Birch, and returns him many thanks for his kind
" present.   He has left an unpublished letter of
" Lord Bacon, which he thinks a valuable one, and
" which he had leave to communicate to Dr. Birch;
" and desires that when he has done with it, he
" would be so good as to send it to Burlington-
" street.

" To the Rev. Dr. Birch.

These notes are preserved in MSS. at the British Museum.

The deputation from Cambridge was attended by the chancellor and a considerable number of members of the university, Drs. Reeve, Akenside, and many other physicians. They were introduced to the King and Queen by the Duke of Newcastle, Chancellor of the University; and to the Princess Dowager by the Duke of Manchester, Lord Chamberlain.

Here we may pause a few moments, to notice a poetical impropriety, on the part of Akenside, not a little curious. He had been admitted, as before stated, to a doctor's degree at Cambridge; but a jealousy subsisting, at that time, between the Universities of Cambridge and Oxford, Akenside, in his HYMN TO THE NAIADS, expressly mentions Cambridge, when his subject required him to mention Oxford:—since Oxford stands upon the Thames; and it is to " The blue-eyed Progeny of Thames," that he addresses himself throughout the whole of his poem.

—————————————— " Tarry, nymphs!
Ye nymphs! ye blue-eyed Progeny of Thames!
Who now the mazes of this rugged heath
Trace with your fleeting steps; who all night long
Repeat amid the cool and tranquil air
Your lonely murmurs, tarry, and receive
My offer'd lay."

The passage, to which I have referred, is this:

> ——————————— " From noon to eve,
> Along the river and the paved brook
> Ascend the cheerful breezes, hail'd of bards,
> Who, *fast by learned Cam*, th' Æolian lyre
> Solicit; nor unwelcome to the youth,
> Who on the heights of Tibur, all inclin'd,
> Or rushing Anio, with a pious hand
> The reverend scene delineates; broken fanes
> Or tombs, or pillar'd aqueducts, the pomp
> Of ancient time; and haply, while he scans
> The ruins, with a silent tear revolves
> The fame and fortune of imperious Rome."

In 1762, Mr. DYSON resigned his clerkship of the House of Commons to Mr. TYRWHITT*, and having been elected Member of Parliament for the borough of Haslemere, he became identified with many of the measures of Lord Bute; as he became afterwards with those of the Duke of Grafton and Lord North.

* This gentleman is well known as the editor of Chaucer, and a part he took in the controversy in regard to Rowley's poems. But he has a higher praise, viz. that arising from his having been the early patron of Dr. Burgess, the present excellent Bishop of Salisbury. " Soon after I had published Dawes's *Miscellanea Critica*," says Dr. Burgess (then Bishop of St. David's, in a letter to Mr. Nichols †) " and was entering

† Dated Aberguilly Palace, March 27, 1815.

Mr. Justice Hardinge, who knew Mr. Dyson well, says, in a letter to Mr. Nichols, that he never saw any thing like the friendship of Mr. Dyson and Dr. Akenside. It extended even to their sentiments; " and yet," says he, " nothing could be more dissimilar than they were. Mr. Dyson was quite a man of business, of order, of parliamentary forms, and of political argument. He had neither fancy nor eloquence; and though he had strong prejudices, he veiled them in obliging manners."

on the term, in which I was to take my master's degree, Mr. Tyrwhitt asked me, ' how I meant to dispose of myself, after I had taken my degree?'   I told him it was my intention to take a curacy in the country, till I should be called again to college to serve those offices, which are usually held by the fellows in rotation.'   He said, ' You must not leave college.   In the country, and with your new duties, you would not have the means and opportunities of pursuing your old studies, which the university possesses above all other places. You shall be *my* curate.   I will beg you to accept, annually, from me what will be equivalent to a curate's stipend.'— I accepted his generous offer," continues the bishop, " and remained at college.   I was soon after appointed to the office of college tutor.   But Mr. Tyrwhitt continued his annual present till the emolument of my office enabled me to relinquish a gratuity, which I knew he would bestow on some protegé, who wanted it more than myself.   The literary advantages, which I derived from my continuing at college, at that time, and, of course, my obligations to my generous friend, are greater than I can express."

N

Sir John Hawkins relates, in his Life of Dr. Johnson, that a person, named SAXBY, who held a situation in the custom-house, and who was of that despicable order, who have the privilege of saying just what they please, was in the constant habit of venting his sarcasms against the medical profession. One evening, says Sir John, this man, after having laboured some time to prove, that the profession of physic was all imposture, turned suddenly upon Akenside—" Doctor," said he, " after all you have said, my opinion of the profession is this :—the ancients endeavoured to make it a science and failed; and the moderns to make it a trade, and succeeded." The company laughed, and Akenside joined in it with good humour.

Sir John relates, also, another anecdote, relative to a low-minded man, named BALLOW. This person was a lawyer of great learning, but of no practice ; full of spleen ; of vulgar manners; and having some connexion with the government, he thought, as many persons, standing in the same relative situation, would have the ignorance to believe, that he was entitled to hate Akenside, for those liberal sentiments, which he seldom thought it necessary either to qualify or to disguise. A dispute, one evening, was the consequence ; and Ballow having made use

of some expressions, little conforming with the
manners of a gentleman, Akenside degraded himself so far as to demand an apology.   On this occasion Akenside seems to have been insensible to the
beauty, and even sublimity, of that sentiment which
teaches, that—

    " Affronts are innocent, when men are worthless."

Ballow was courageous enough to insult, but not
sufficiently so to pay the penalty.   He, therefore,
screened himself from punishment by keeping out
of the way.   Akenside's anger soon subsided; and
then some mutual friends adjusted the difference.
Sir John seems disposed to cast an air of ridicule
over Akenside's conduct in this matter; but to
challenge a man, like Ballow, must have been in
itself a punishment to the sensitive mind of Akenside, in itself sufficient, for having given way to a
weakness so unworthy a poet of high rank, and
more especially a philosopher of no mean order.

    Few men ever lived, who had a greater inward
detestation of tyranny and bigotry, than Akenside.
This feeling is indicated in all his poems; and he
had an equal contempt for hypocrisy.   Considering, with Shaftesbury *, that the Deity was the

    * Characteristics, ii. 294.

sovereign source of all beauty, he was always indignant, when the name of that most wonderful
Being was alluded to in a gross, vulgar, or indif-
ferent manner. "People would assert," he was
accustomed to say, " that I imitated Newton, or I
should never allude to the Deity, or hear him alluded
to by others, but I should make an inclination of
my body." And one day, being in company with
Mr. Meyrick's father at a coffee-house, in the
neighbourhood of Charing-cross, having listened,
for some time, with impatience to the oratory of a
Mr. Warnefield, who was making some severe remarks not only on Warburton's Divine Legation of
Moses, but on the Bible itself, he, at length, interrupted him. " I tell you what, sir," said he;
" Warburton is no friend of mine;—but I detest
hearing a man of learning abused. As to the Bible
—believe or not, just as you please; but let it contain as many absurdities, untruths, and unsound
doctrines, as you say it does, there is one passage,
at least, that I am sure, you, with all your ingenuity,
and with all the eloquence you possess, have not the
power to surpass. It is where the prophet says,
' The children of men are much wiser than the
children of light.'"

And here I take pleasure in citing a passage sent

to me by an octogenarian of great learning, who
assures me, that he has every reason to think,
that it formed part of a letter from Akenside
to Dr. Grainger, author of the Sugar Cane *.
" Your friend seems to doubt whether he has a
soul or not; and yet surely he will not attempt to
place himself on a level with Kepler; and so far
was he from doubting, that he had a soul, he gives
one even to the earth itself †." " In respect to its
nature," said he, on another occasion, " it is past
my judgment, whether material or immaterial.
Perhaps it may partake of both natures. Tertul-
lian not only makes the soul material ‡, but he gives

* " Grainger," says Dr. Percy, Bishop of Dromore, " was
not only a man of learning, but of excellent virtue; one of
the most friendly, generous, and benevolent men I ever
knew." Grainger's Georgic is now chiefly known by the
tale of Junio and Theana. There are, however, some fine
passages in it; and many beautiful descriptions of tropical
vegetation.

† Probably, Akenside alluded to the following passage:—
" *Denique terræ globus tale corpus erit, quale est alicujus
animalis : quidque animali est sua anima, hoc erit telluri
hæc, quam quærimus, natura sublunaris.*"

‡ " Nos autem animam corporalem, et hic profitemur, et
in suo volumine probamus habentem proprium genus sub-
stantiæ, et soliditatis, per quam quid, et sentire, et pati
possit."—" Quis negavit Deum esse corpus."

a corporal body even to God himself; and Job says, ' In my flesh I shall see God.' The Christian doctrine, also, implies it; since it speaks of the resurrection of the body. Certainly, every thing that exists must have shape; and if shape, form; and if form, substance. But there may be many substances, and no doubt there are, beyond what we know of at present. Simplicius says, there is in nature an active principle and a passive one: the soul may partake of the same differences; the former principle, associating with light; the latter with colour. Maximus Tyrius makes even a bolder assertion; for, he says, that God's oracles and men's understandings are of near alliance. Hence the assertion of Proclus, that all our souls are the children of God. But the fact is, we know little of these things. It is a great satisfaction, however, that we live in a world, presenting, every moment, something to exercise our faculties; and that the grand mover of the whole will, no doubt, make ample allowances for human infirmity."

Akenside, however, seldom conversed on subjects of this kind. They are very dangerous for medical men to touch upon. The religious creed of Akenside, if we may judge by his poem, seems to have associated

with that of Lord Shaftesbury*,—pure theism : but
that he had a high respect for the Christian Reve-
lation, and a profound reverence for the Christian
doctrine, is very evident from his ode to the Bishop
of Winchester, and that to the author of the Memoirs of the House of Brandenburg.   There is,
perhaps, a still more striking proof of his respect for
Christianity.   For, when a boy, I remember hearing Sir Grey Cooper, Bart., read a paraphrase of the
Benedicite, which, he told my father, was written
by Akenside.   " I know it has been attributed to
other persons," said Sir Grey, " but I have very
good reasons for believing, that it was written by
Akenside ; and I am proud of it ; for Akenside was
a townsman of mine ; and I remember hearing, that
he was, also, author of one of the Christmas Carols †

---

* See Characteristics, ii. 11, 71, 72, 73, 74, 267, 268, 358.
—Ed. 1737.

† Mr. Brand alludes to Carols of this kind in his observations on Popular Antiquities.   (See Ellis's edition, vol. i.
350, 4to.)   " J. Boemus Aubanus tells us, that in Franconia,
on the three Thursday nights of our Lord, it is customary
for the youth of both sexes to go from house to house,
knocking at the doors, singing their Christmas Carols, and
wishing a happy new year.   They get, in return, at the
houses, they stop at, pears, apples, nuts, and even money.

" Little troops of boys and girls still go about, in this very
manner, at Newcastle-upon-Tyne, and other places in the

which used to be sung about the streets of Newcastle many years ago." This paraphrase we do not
venture, however, to insert; since, had it really been
written by Akenside, it would, assuredly, have been
inserted in Mr. Dyson's edition of 1772. It is too
beautiful to have been omitted.

SIR GREY COOPER was born at Newcastle-upon-
Tyne, and was bred to the profession of a barrister;
and a speech still remains upon record, delivered by
him at the bar of the House of Commons, which
may perhaps be cited as one of the best, ever delivered on a mere local subject *. He wrote a
pamphlet, entitled " *A Pair of Spectacles for Short-
sighted Politicians*," which had the good fortune to
recommend him to the ministry of the day; and he
became, subsequently, Member of Parliament for
the borough of Sandwich, and Secretary to the

north of England, some few nights before, on the night of
the eve of Christmas-day, and on that of the day itself.
The Hagmena (as it is called) is still preserved among them,
and they always conclude their begging song with wishing
a merry Christmas, and a happy new year."

* " State of the proceedings in the House of Commons on
the petition of the DUKE and DUCHESS of ATHOLL, against
the Bill, ' for the more effectually preventing the mischiefs
arising to the revenue and commerce of Great Britain and
Ireland, from the illicit and clandestine trade to and from
the ISLE OF MAN.' "

Treasury, during the whole administration of Lord North. His use to that minister, on particular occasions, is thus illustrated in the correspondence of Sir John Sinclair *.

" LORD NORTH was often lulled into a profound sleep by the omniferous oratory of some of the parliamentary speakers. SIR GREY COOPER (one of the Secretaries of the Treasury), meanwhile took notes of the principal arguments of his opponents, which, by glancing his eye over the paper, Lord North was enabled immediately to answer. On a naval question, a member thought proper to give an historical detail of the origin and progress of ship-building, which he deduced from Noah's Ark, and in regular order brought down to the Spanish Armada. Sir Grey, inadvertently, awoke his lordship at this period; who asked, to what era the honourable gentleman had arrived? Being told, ' to the reign of Queen Elizabeth,' he instantly replied, ' Dear Sir Grey, why did you not let me sleep a century or two more?' "

On the resignation of Lord North, Sir Grey retired into private life. Having spent all the earlier part of my life in the village and neighbourhood to which he retired, I had many opportunities of seeing and conversing with him. He had a small temple or summer-house, in a remote part of the village, called the HALL-GROVE. This summer-house was

* Vol. i. p. 76.

generally kept unlocked, and every one might go into it that pleased. I frequently availed myself of this liberty; and one day found a copy of Akenside, which had been left on the table by one of Sir Grey's family; and seating myself on a small parapet, overhung with jessamine, honey-suckles, and clematis, opened the book, and imbibed, for the first time, that ardent admiration of the works of this poet, which has continued through life, and led at last to the presumption of endeavouring to illustrate his life, writings, and genius*.

Sir Grey was rather haughty, when displeased; but the most condescending of men, when in good humour. He had great dignity in his deportment; was of a kind and humane disposition; and one of the best and most indulgent of parents. One day my father charged me with the deliverance of a letter, when Sir Grey took me into his private apartment, and presented me with a copy of two poems, he had printed for the use of his friends. One of these I presume to insert,—either out of gratitude or resentment,—for having first awakened

---

* Bowles. "The influence of the imagination, on the conduct of life, is one of the most important points in moral philosophy. It were easy, by an induction of facts, to prove, that the imagination directs almost all the passions, and mixes with almost every circumstance of action or pleasure."
—*Akenside.*

in me an ambition to be remembered a few short days beyond the hour of death.

" TO THE NYMPH OF THE FOUNTAIN OF TEARS.

" HAIL, pious nymph! whose guardian power
 The holy spring of Tears protects,
And each soft drop and tender shower
 From the mysterious source directs:

" Not tears, that, on th' approach of death,
 Down the pale cheek of tyrants roll,
When Conscience, to the latest breath,
 Holds up the mirror to the soul:

" Nor such as moisten the dark cells
 Where, midst the slaves the rack prepare,
The stern inquisitor compels
 E'en godlike virtue to despair.

" These bitter waters of distress
 Arise from other springs than thine;
Springs, which infernal gnomes possess,
 Dread ministers of wrath divine!

" Heaven gives to thee the sacred part
 Of watching the pure streams, that flow
From the soft motions of the heart,
 That learns to feel another's woe:

" To raise the head by care depress'd,
 With gentle, delicate, relief;
To pour into the wounded breast
 The balm of sympathetic grief.—

" Such soothing offices engage
    Thy sylphs, the messengers of grace,
Sent by thy order to assuage
    The sorrows of the human race.

" To thee belong the gushing rills
    Of sudden joy and glad surprise,
The rapt soul's transport, that distils
    Glistening in th' expressive eyes.

" Let me, thy suppliant, take my part
    In all thy pleasures, all thy pains;
And ne'er, though exquisite the smart,
    Of sensibility complain :

" Oft let me leave the busy scene,
    Devotion at thy shrine to pay ;
Oft taste with thee the calm serene
    Evening of a well-spent day ;

" And, in thy grotto's hallow'd shade,
    Gaze at the children of the world,
In vanity's light barks convey'd,
    With every glittering sail unfurl'd :

" Smile at the GREAT, for what they choose
    In each fond wish and fickle mood ;
And pity them for what they lose—
    The power divine of doing good.

" View the mild glory round the throne,
    Love with obedience command ;
For other's rights maintain its own,
    And rule to bless a grateful land.

" To cheer me in the vale of tears,
    Still, pensive nymph! thy grace impart,
Still let thy spring of tender tears
    Enlarge and purify my heart;

" For with those social feelings glow
    The best affections of the mind;
The warmth of friendship, and the glow
    Of charity to all mankind*."

---

* The following letters, which have lately appeared in the Garrick correspondence, are important in more lights than one :—

                                " Tuesday morning.

" MY DEAR GARRICK,

        " I GIVE you my most cordial thanks for the delight I received last night; and Lord NORTH commands me to express his obligation to you in the strongest manner. I cannot go in comfort to my wife and children at Windsor, till I am assured, that you have not suffered for this inimitable exertion of your powers. I never remember to have seen or heard you greater, *tam in concitatis quam in remissis affectibus,* which Quintilian says of Cicero in one of his finest orations. I beg my compliments to Mrs. Garrick. I saw her stooping from her cloud and gazing at you. I thought the spirit of Shakspeare was, probably, doing the same, and with equal applause. By the by, why should not those fine lines, in the Essay on Man, be applied to your demi-god, as well as Newton?

    ' Superior beings, when of late they saw
    A mortal man unfold all nature's law,' &c.

    " I am, my dear sir, very affectionately yours,
                    " GREY COOPER."

Among the friends of Akenside may be, also, mentioned Mr. WRAY; to whom Mr. Edwards ad-

" Parliament Street, March 14, 1771.

" MY DEAR SIR,

" I WILL not fail to use my best endeavours to obtain what you request, and I am well assured, that LORD NORTH will receive the application with a favourable impression, as it comes from you. At the same time I must acquaint you, that the same indulgence, which Mr. R. Burke desires, was, last year, refused to Mr. Haliday, the collector of Antigua, on the ground of his having been only one year attending his duty, since his former leave of absence expired. This is the very case of Mr. Richard Burke; but as my heart always inclines me to go beyond the severe rules of my duty, in soliciting the petitions of the lowest officers of the crown, when they apply for leave of absence on account of their health, or the urgency of their private affairs, even when the facts do not come so well vouched, as they ought to be by the rules of office, I cannot refuse my assistance to the recommendations of a friend, whom upon much greater occasions I should be happy to oblige. *Lord North is the best-natured man in the world,* and I know, he will as readily do a favour, or grant a reasonable indulgence, to the brother of Mr. E. Burke, as to any of those who stand in the rank of his political friends. Nothing but public consideration, and the tendency of the example, can prevent him from granting what is requested.

" I am, my dear sir, with the truest regard, your very faithful servant,

" GREY COOPER."

ENDORSED,

" Sir Grey Cooper. March 17, 1771.
    " Richard Burke."

dressed a sonnet, peculiarly characteristic of their different fortunes in life.

> " *Treasury Chambers.*
> " *March* 18, 1771.

" DEAR SIR,

" I HAVE the pleasure (because I know it will give you pleasure) to acquaint you, that I have obtained Lord North's permission to order a warrant for granting leave of absence to Mr. Richard Burke for one year.

" By some expressions in your last letter, you seem to misunderstand what I wrote to you. I never conceived, that *any gentleman should be refused an ordinary and reasonable indulgence on account of his political conduct; much less that of his relations.* The warrant will, I hope, be signed to-morrow.

" I am, my dear sir, yours ever most faithfully,

" GREY COOPER."

> " *Parliament Street, Nov.* 8, 1771.

" MY DEAR SIR,

" I HAVE received your letter this morning, and sent it to LADY NORTH. She and my lord must be much pleased with the polite offer you make them of your charming villa; though I should suppose, that my lord's business (which grows upon him every hour we get nearer to parliament) will not suffer him to avail himself of it. I attended her ladyship and my wife last night to the play. How I was mortified that I did not see you, and how grieved for the cause of your absence! I beg to know particularly how you do : I would have waited upon you, if I had not been still very lame, of a sprained ancle. Mr. R. Burke has called on me, and I have returned his visit. JUNIUS writes again to-day both in the shape of a letter and a card.

" Wray, whose dear friendship in the dawning years
    Of undesigning childhood first began,
    Though youth's gay morn with even tenour ran,
My noon conducted, and my evening cheers,

" With regard to the subject of your former letter, *my
constant conduct and language have been, that though, in reading the letters, I was often led to conjecture and to believe,
that they were written by that person*, I as often felt myself
restrained and controlled from entertaining such suspicions,
by the solemn declarations, and the parole of the honour of a
gentleman, which I had heard from you he had given, and
which every* GENTLEMAN HOLDS MORE SACRED THAN HIS
LIFE.

    " I am, my dear sir, yours most truly,
                      " Grey Cooper."

MR. GARRICK TO SIR GREY COOPER.

                    " *Adelphi, Feb.* 1, 1774.

" MY DEAR SIR,

       " It is not possible for me to believe, what my
servant tells me, nay I should scarce have believed my own
eyes, had I seen it. He tells me, that you in company with
a certain lord, whom I most honour and would soonest obey,
called yesterday at the Adelphi! Impossible! I beg and
beseech you, my good friend, not to make me too vain; but
if there are any commands to either of the Indies; if it is

---

  * Mr. Edward Burke. Since Sir Grey entertained this
opinion, it is most probable, that Lord North did the same;
and there are few things more remarkable in the history of
that mystery.

Rightly dost thou, in whom combined appears,
   Whate'er for public life completes the man,
   With native zeal strike out a larger plan,
No useless friends of senators and peers;
   Me talents moderate, and small estate,
   Fit for retirement's unambitious shade.
Nor envy I, who ne'er approach the throne,
   But joyful see thee mingle with the great,
And praise my lot, contented with my own *."

---

thought proper that I should be commander-in-chief; or if I should be fixed to make the Bostonians drink tea, as they ought, or send them after the tea into the Atlantic,—pray let me know directly, that I may resign the kingdoms of England and Scotland, in the persons of Richard the Third and Macbeth, and prepare to go any where, as that noble lord should be pleased to command me.

    " I am your most obliged and obedient,

              " D. GARRICK."

Reply.

" MY DEAR SIR,

    " THE wit and pleasantry of your letter have delighted us all. Lord North cannot afford, either on the account of his taste or his popularity, to send the favourite of the nation to such barbarous places as Bengal or Boston. He hopes, however, that you will soon prove, that you have neither abdicated nor deserted the kingdoms of Scotland or England.

    " Ever yours most faithfully,

              " GREY COOPER."

* The character of Mr. Wray is thus sketched by Mr. Justice Hardinge.

O

Akenside having completed, in 1765, the second
book of his new poem on the Imagination, took

" It may appear, at the first glance of it, a paradox, but,
I believe, it will be found correct, when it is analysed,
and compared with experience, to say, that nothing is more
difficult than to give the portrait of a *singular* man;—I
mean the features and the countenance of his mind. I shall,
therefore, only attempt a faint impression of a *deportment*
and of a *manner*, the most original, that I ever knew.

" Mr. WRAY had a vivacity, and laughing air, half ludi-
crous, yet exciting no ridicule, and bordering upon levity,
but never too near it—more juvenile at least than his age;
but in this comic humour he was never coarse, or ill-bred;
was never too free, and never ill-natured. He was blessed
with a power *to make instruction pleasant*, which no colours
can reach.

" I have known men of distinguished parts, and wit, who
seem to have got by heart a whole string of epigrams in
prose, and *bon mots*, to be let off in the course of the day.
Shakspeare, who was at home in every human character, and
walked in every path of it, says of those men, as represented
by one of his dramatic figures,

> ' This fellow picks up wit, as pigeons pease,
>   And utters it again, as Jove doth please.'

" Horace describes the jester of his day :

> ——————————————————— ' *facetos*
> Qui *captat* risus hominum, famamque dicacis.'

" Mr. Wray had no such ambition; he was above it: all
his whims of thought, fancy, or expression, were not only
his own, but were prompted by the casual impulse of the

occasion, the following year, to read it to Lord and Lady Dacre, at their seat, called Mount Ararat. This circumstance is related by Mr. Wray in a letter to one of his friends *. " I was at Mount Ararat to attend *Lord and Lady Dacre*, accompanied by *Akenside*, who passed the evening there, and communicated the second and part of a third book in his great work. In the former, and in the

* Sept. 23, 1766.

---

moment. He had a right even to be as dull, as he was brilliant, from his perfect indifference to the effect of all, that he said, except that he was happy in communicating pleasure to those around him.

" In general society he had no imperious air of the pedant, or fopperies of taste. He had no oracles to deliver ; no *little senate* for his *laws;* but ' *spared his own strength* †,' in wisdom or in wit. He had a light and familiar note, that made its party good with boys and girls. He rather said in a lively and comic style what carried the weight of a powerful intellect, than what are foolishly called ' *good things.*'

" I can remember a thousand *bons mots* of those *wits professed*, CHESTERFIELD, HORACE WALPOLE, and SELWYN. Of Wray, I recollect none : and it is not because they did not exist ; it is because they were melted into something better and superior."—*Nichols' Illustrations.*

---

† Parcentibus viribus.—*Hor.*

same philosophical way, he is eloquent on the topics of truth and virtue, vice and the passions. In the latter, Solon is introduced giving a fable on *the origin of evil.* It is introduced by an episode from *Herodotus* of *Argavista's Marriage,* the *daughter of Clisthenes,* which is delightfully poetical."

In 1768 Akenside published three essays in the Medical Transactions. 1. On Cancers; 2. On the Use of Ipecacuanha in Asthmas; 3. On the best Method of treating White Swellings of the Joints.

1. In the first he gives an instance of a cancer in utero, which was cured by the cicuta and the bark; one, in which a cancer in the tongue was cured by the cicuta, corrosive sublimate, and the bark; and a third, in which a cancered lip was cured in the same manner; with this difference, that the cicuta, having removed the pains, which was all that could be expected from it, was laid aside at the end of ten days.

2. In respect to asthmas, Akenside directs, that where the indisposition is chronical and habitual, from three to five grains of ipecacuanha every morning. "The effects," says the author, "do not depend on exercise, or the action of vomiting; but upon the antispasmodic virtues of ipecacoan."

3. In regard to white swellings of the joints,

Akenside recommends the application of a blister round the part affected; which he directs to be kept open, and reduced to such a size, as the nature of the complaint may seem to require: but nothing, he adds, is to be expected from this treatment, when there is any sensible collection of fluid within the joint.

Having been appointed Krohnian Lecturer, Akenside chose for his subject the History of the Revival of Learning; and he read three lectures on that comprehensive theme before the College of Physicians. But some of the members having justly remarked, that the subject was foreign to the purposes of that institution, he declined proceeding farther.

About the same period he read an account of some observations, he had made at St. Thomas's Hospital, on the putrid erysipelas. These observations he intended for the second volume of the Medical Transactions; but death prevented their publication *.

* It has been generally believed that there are several MSS. of Akenside at the College of Physicians, or at the College of Surgeons. This, however, is not the fact; as may be seen by the following letters :—

I shall now say something of my old and respected friend, Mr. Meyrick.   He lived in Swallow-street many years, and died at Hammersmith in 1807. When I was first introduced to him, which was in the early part of that year, he shook me so cordially by the hand, at parting, that it ached for many minutes afterwards.   He was, nevertheless, far from

> " *Royal College of Surgeons, Oct.* 17, 1831.
>
> " SIR,
>
> " In reply to your letter of yesterday I have to acquaint you that I do not find, among the papers, preserved at this College, any MSS. or memoranda whatever, relating to Dr. Akenside.
>
> > " I am, Sir,
> > " Your most obedient humble servant,
> > > " EDMUND BELFOUR."

> " *College of Physicians, Oct.* 2d, 1831.
>
> " SIR,
>
> " I am requested by SIR HENRY HALFORD, President of the Royal College of Physicians, to inform you that there are no MSS. or other papers relating to Dr. Akenside, to be found in the College Library; and to assure you, that had there been any such, every facility of access to them would have been readily afforded to you.
>
> > " I have the honour to be, Sir,
> > > " Your obedient servant,
> > > > " FRANCIS HAWKINS, M. D.
>
> " *To Charles Bucke, Esq.*"

being rough or rude in his manners. He was, on the contrary, good-nature itself. He had a great dislike to be thought to have more information, than he really had, and was strongly averse to any thing like authorship. " I have known many authors," he would say, " but I never saw any thing in their fortunes or physiognomies to envy." " I 'll tell you a witty saying of mine," said he, one day. " GLOVER came once into my shop; and putting a prescription into my hand, desired me to make it up for him. ' I think I am coming to a *sad pass*,' said he; ' my health declines daily.' ' No,' said I; ' no, sir, you are not yet come to a *sad pass;* for if you were, you could not have made Leonidas fight so gallantly at the *pass of Thermopylæ.*' Glover," continued he, " was one of the best men I ever knew. Some people want us to believe, that he wrote Junius's letters. Why, he was a friend of Mr. Dyson; could he, therefore, write of Mr. Dyson as Junius did? Besides, the Duke of Bedford had done him several small pieces of service. It is a libel upon human nature to suppose such a thing."

Junius, indeed, wrote very irreverendly of Mr. Dyson. Soon after his resignation of the clerkship of the House of Commons, Mr. Dyson was appointed

Secretary to the Treasury.   In 1768 he was appointed one of the Lords of the Treasury, under the Duke of Grafton, in conjunction with Lord North (Chancellor of the Exchequer), Mr. Onslow, the once celebrated Charles Jenkinson, and Mr. Charles Townsend.   He does not appear to have been a very eloquent debater, nor indeed a frequent speaker: but his opinions were always characterised by plain, practical, common sense;   and as his name must always command great respect, and even reverence, for the magnificence of his conduct to Akenside, the insertion of one of his speeches, by way of specimen, cannot fail to be interesting.

" *Jan.* 9, 1770.—We have been told, sir, in a laboured harangue (from Mr. Serjeant Glynn), that we have lost the love and confidence of the people ; that an honourable gentleman, who has reproached us with betraying our trust, has spoken the sentiments of the people ; that we are, at this moment, in danger of being called to an account by the people ; that the people are ready to do themselves justice upon us ; and that we should be aware what we do, because the people, whom, by one of those rhetorical flourishes, which are so useful, on other occasions, he calls the *avenger*, is at the door.   Sir, it is hard to say, whether this insult is more gross against this house, or the people.   Is the rabble, that is now supposed to be gathered about the door, the people? Are the writers of the newspapers, who wish for a prison or the pillory, that their libels may be thought more important, the people? The people are too great, too respectable a body, to become the tool, the puppet of any faction. They are not to be hired to halloo and hiss with porter and geneva; they are not to be brought gaping to an inn, by such tricks and devices, as gull clowns at a fair. An honourable gentleman has told us, that he did not seek petitioners; but that petitioners sought him :—but it is well known, that though this may be true in appearance, it is false in fact. When a great man has a mind to be thus sought, intimations are given to proper persons, that they must seek him; a few stanch friends meet together, with an invitation to the great man, drawn up by himself, in their pocket. When this is formally sent to him, he graciously vouchsafes to attend. A general meeting is then proposed; advertisements are inserted in the newspapers; cards of invitation are every where distributed; and agents attend on market days at inns and alehouses, to see, who can be picked up by the influence of a customer, or the hopes of a treat. The great man receives another copy of the invitation to himself; and he again deigns to accept it. When he comes, he is pressed to take the chair, as has been preconcerted, and thus he is happily sought and found. From the chair he relates what he has heard from the minority of this house, of wicked ministers and injured liberty; taking care to suppress the arguments, by which the majority support the wisdom of parliament and the rectitude of administration ; and then, producing a petition, hands are collected, like money at the church-door for a brief ; and when this rhapsody of malice and sedition, in which majesty and ministry are involved in one general charge of combining against the constitution, is brought up to insult the king and disgrace government, we are told it is the sense of the people ! We have been superciliously warned of tyranny, and told, that it is advancing against us in hasty strides. I am an enemy to tyranny, sir ; and, therefore, I cannot without indignation hear this house threatened with the most preposterous and horrid of all tyranny, that of a mob. To insinuate, that the measures of a legislative body should be influenced by echoes of sedition from the rabble, is to insinuate, that all government should be at an end. It is to restrain those, with whose vengeance we are now threatened, that all government is instituted ; and if they are not restrained, a state of nature will return, and the earth will be filled with violence and oppression, under the pretence of liberty and justice. If our liberties are in danger, it is from those, who have set up the cry ; it is from those, who insult both majesty and administration ; and not from those who would support the best of princes, in the exercise of constitutional rites, and the measures to which he gives the sanction of his authority."

Jan. 26, 1769.—Mr. Dyson spoke in favour of Lord North's measures, in regard to America.

March 15, 1770.—He spoke on the subject of

the Remonstrance of the city of London to the king.

March 28 (same year).—He spoke against Mr. Grenville's bill for regulating the trials of contested elections.

Feb. 27, 1771.—He spoke against a bill, introduced to repeal a clause in the act for quieting the possession of the subject, called the nullum tempest act.

April 25, 1771.—He spoke on the Shoreham bill: and on *March* 2, 1773, he delivered his sentiments in favour of the bill, introduced by Sir Henry Hoghton, for the further relief of his majesty's protestant subjects, dissenting from the church of England.

These are all the instances, recorded, in which Mr. Dyson took any prominent part in the debates of the house; but as debates were not published in those times, in the manner they are at present; it is impossible now to ascertain how frequently he otherwise spoke, on what subjects, and to what purport.

In February, 1770, we find him resigning his situation of a Lord of the Admiralty in favour of Mr. Fox, upon a pension being granted him on the Irish establishment, for his own life and those of his

three sons. This pension, however, he did not enjoy quite two years. It was taken up in the Irish
house of parliament, upon the ground of its being
an unnecessary charge upon that country; and on
a division Mr. Dyson lost his pension by a majority of one *. On this occasion Mr. FLOOD made
one of those furious attacks, for which he was so
greatly remarkable. " Of all the burthens which
it has pleased government to lay upon our devoted
shoulders," said Mr. Flood, " that, which is the
subject of the present debate, is the most grievous
and intolerable. Who does not know Jeremiah
Dyson, Esq.? We know little of him indeed,
otherwise than by his name in our pension list; but
there are others, who know him by his actions.
This is he, who is endued with those happy talents,
that he has served every administration, and served
every one with equal success,—a civil, pliable, good-
natured gentleman, who will do what you will, and
say what you please, for payment."

Mr. Flood was here interrupted. " The honourable gentleman," said a member, " ought to pay
more respect to Mr. Dyson, as one of his majesty's
officers, and, as such, on whom his majesty was
graciously pleased to repose confidence in."

* Nov. 25, 1771.

" As to the royal confidence," answered Mr. Flood, " reposed in Mr. Dyson, his gracious majesty (whom God long preserve) has been graciously lavish of it, not only to Mr. Dyson, but to the friends of Mr. Dyson ; and I think the choice was good : the royal secrets will, I dare say, be very secure in their breasts, not only for the love they bear to his gracious majesty, but for the love they bear themselves. In the present case, however, we do not want to be informed of that part of Mr. Dyson's character—we know enough of him,— every body knows enough of him. Ask the British treasury—the British council—ask any Englishman who he is, what he is,—they can all tell you, for the gentleman is well known. But what have we to do with him ? He never served Ireland, nor the friends of Ireland. And if this distressed kingdom was never benefited by his counsel, interest, or service, I see no reason why this kingdom should reward him ! Let the honourable members of this house consider this, and give their voices accordingly. For God's sake, let every man consult his conscience :—If Jeremiah Dyson, Esq. shall be found to deserve this pension, let it be continued; if not, let it be lopped off our revenue as burthensome and unnecessary."

In respect to politics, it is wise to pass no judgments. Like every other man, Mr. Dyson had a
right to think for himself. For my own part I have
seen so many patriotic talkers tyrants in their own
fields, houses, circles, and neighbourhoods; and so
many advocates for aristocratical power mild, gentle,
and conciliating, that I have long ceased to form
judgments of men, grounded on the questionable
basis of political opinion. Mr. Dyson thought for
himself, and acted for himself. As a private character, he appears to have been highly estimable.
" He was an excellent father," says Mr. Hatsell,
who dedicated to him the second volume of his
precedents of the proceedings of the House of Commons; " of comprehensive knowledge, acuteness of
understanding, and inflexible integrity, great knowledge of history in general, and of the laws and
constitution of this country in particular." As the
friend and patron of Akenside he must always be
reverenced, and can never be forgotten *.

* Mr. Dyson survived his friend rather more than six
years. He died Sept. 16, 1776, universally respected and
beloved. At the time of his death, he was M. P. for Hors-
ham, a member of the Privy Council, and cofferer to the
household of George the third.
There are two letters, still extant, in MS., in which Mr.
Dyson is mentioned, from the celebrated ADAM SMITH to

The whole correspondence of Akenside with Mr. Dyson, if preserved, would have been, doubtless,

Dr. ROEBUCK of Birmingham. These letters are very remarkable;—not so much as they respect Mr. Dyson, as they are in regard to the methods, which they develope, pursued by the administration (of which Mr. Dyson was a member), in respect to the British colonies in America.

"MY DEAR FRIEND,

"This letter is wrote to you in perfect confidence, and at the particular desire of a man of very considerable consequence in this country. The contents of it must be kept as secret as possible, even tho' you should be disposed to comply with the proposal. If, after having read and maturely considered it, you should not be disposed to comply with it, I will beg the favour of you to *throw it in the fire.*

"By the latest accounts from the Congress in America, it appears, that the Deputies from Maryland, New York, Pensylvania, and New Hampshire, all firmly opposed a non-importation agreement as absurd and ineffectual; *they proposed to try the interest of the Colonies in England, by sending a deputation with a petition to the King and Parliament;* and to endeavour to accommodate matters with the mother country, in the best manner that they could. This measure was likely to be adopted, when letters arrived from Dr. Franklin, recommending a non-importation agreement, as the measure most likely to interest the merchants of England in their favour, and to *bring petitions to Parliament from all the principal manufacturing towns, praying a repeal of the late acts,* relating to the town of Boston, and colony of Massachusset's Bay. These letters altered entirely the disposition

a high treat to the intellectual reader. Only a small portion of that correspondence, however, re-

of the Congress. The deputies of New York, however, being convinced of the impropriety of the non-importation agreement, but not being able to prevent it, were endeavouring to evade it by modifying it. A general non-importation agreement was allowed, on all hands, to be absurd; as there were some commodities, which they could not do without. These necessary commodities were not the same in all the different colonies. It was necessary, therefore, to regulate what commodities should be excluded only from certain colonies. This was the state of the debates when the last letters came away.

" In the mean time, Franklin's agents, assisted by some of the worst and most unprincipled members of the opposition, have been extremely active in some of the principal manufacturing towns of the North, particularly among the dissenters, to prepare the people for making and supporting such petitions.

" There is nothing so much wanted, at present, as a man of known probity, candour, and judgment, and of established credit and authority in these towns, *who would take some pains to explain to the principal people the nature and probable effects of this scheme; that it is in reality nothing less, than an infamous conspiracy to dismember the British empire.*

" If, under pretence of your own private business, you could undertake, as soon as possible, for there is very little time to lose, a journey through Manchester, Birmingham, Leeds, Sheffield, &c., and, on seeing your friends, explain to them, in a proper manner, the real state of the case, you would be received here, by the principal members of administration,

mains; and this, it is hoped, will be, one day, given to the world.

as a person, who had rendered the most important service to the state.

" If there was any hope, that we should ever see your friend DYSON in the state of health, in which you left him, there is nothing, I am sure, would give him so much pleasure, or increase so much, if that be possible, the cordial esteem he has always had for you. By the accounts I had from his house to-day, I find he continues better, and, it is to be hoped, is out of immediate danger, but still not what he was.

" Franklin said, some years ago, in the presence of a particular friend of mine, with much triumph, that whatever measures Great Britain might choose to pursue, with regard to her colonies, whether mild or vigorous, they would equally tend to bring about this great and desirable event of the entire independency of America. Be assured, that this is his determined purpose; which to his friends, he makes no scruple of avowing. Will you suffer your friends to be made the tools of this* the worst citizen I ever knew in Great Britain.

" I received, some weeks ago, a letter from Mr. Johnson. His project lies a little out of my road, as I know few mercantile people here. Diligent inquiry, however, neither has been, nor shall be wanting. I shall write to him, as soon as I know with certainty, whether I can or cannot be of any

---

* The following words are lined in the MS.—*" proud, supercilious, and malignant knave, without any exception, the worst citizen,"* &c.

P

" *Newgrove, Petworth, Oct.* 7, 1831.

" SIR,

" I received yesterday from my son your letter, requesting ' to be informed whether Dr.

use to him. Remember me to Mrs. Roebuck and to all the young gentlemen, and let me hear from you soon.

" I ever am, my dear friend,

" Most faithfully yours,

(Signed) " A. SMITH.

" *Suffolk Street, Charing Cross, No.* 27.

" *17th Nov.* 1774."

" MY DEAR FRIEND,

" I shall begin this letter with a circumstance, which I am sure, will be agreeable. Your friend, Mr. DYSON, is in a fair way towards a complete recovery. He sits up the greater part of the day; his spirits are very good, and his judgment, memory, and speech are all restored.

" Your letter of the 28th of November, I communicated to the Solicitor-general *, who desired leave to keep it for some days, till he had an opportunity of showing it to Lord North, and conversing with him at leisure on the subject. His lordship, as well as my friend, expressed the highest satisfaction at the honest zeal which your letter expressed, as well as the highest confidence in the prudence, with which they expect you will conduct this business. They both consider themselves, as well as the state, as under very par-

---

* Mr. Wedderburne, afterwards Lord Loughborough.

Akenside had left any papers, that could be interesting to his ' numerous appreciators and admirers.'

" I have only some letters from him to my father, in the early period of their friendship (from 1742 to 1745), which I looked at yesterday evening. There are passages in them which show the warmth of his heart, the extent of his classical knowledge, and the highness of his mind. But I doubt whether they would now interest the public ; and as my father never communicated them to any editor of his friend's life, you will think me justified in following his example.

ficular obligations to you ; and, when you come to town, will be very happy in any opportunity of expressing their sense of so important a service. Leeds, I find, is the town that is most suspected, and where the discontented party have been making the greatest efforts to procure petitions. If petitions cannot be prevented altogether, the expedient, you propose, of counter-petitions is certainly the best. I shall be very happy to hear from you in the course of your journey.

" I ever am, my dear sir,

" most faithfully yours,

(Signed) " A. SMITH.

" *Suffolk Street, No.* 27, *Charing Cross,*
" *9th Dec.* 1774."

" With every acknowledgment of the terms in which you speak of my father,

　　　　" I remain, Sir,

　　　　　　" Your obedient servant,

　　　　　　　　　" J. DYSON.

" *Charles Bucke, Esq.*"

Akenside was a great admirer of Gothic architecture. " I have occasionally caught him," said Mr. Meyrick, " contemplating with great earnestness the exterior of Westminster Abbey. He would frequently sit, of a fine moonlight night, on the benches in St. James's Park, gazing on that sublime structure; and I remember he once told me, that he seldom thought of the passage in his own poem,

　' The radiant sun, the moon's nocturnal lamp,' &c.

but he thought of a still finer one in Pope's Homer.

' As when the moon, refulgent lamp of light !
　O'er heaven's clear azure spreads her sacred light ;
　When not a breath disturbs the deep serene,
　And not a cloud o'ercasts the solemn scene ;
　Around her throne the vivid planets roll,
　And stars, unnumber'd, gild the glowing pole ;
　O'er the dark trees a yellower verdure shed,
　And tip with silver every mountain's head ;
　Then shine the vales, the rocks in prospect rise,
　And floods of glory burst from all the skies.' "

And this reminds me of BLOOMFIELD, author of that immortal GEORGIC, " THE FARMER's BOY." He was a great admirer of Akenside. " There are many parts of his great poem," said he to me, one day, as we were walking together in his humble garden, near the Shepherd and Shepherdess fields, " that I do not comprehend; but what I do understand, I cannot express my admiration of. I never read his poem till after I had written my own; but I think I must have somewhere seen this passage :—

———————————————— 'Some to higher hopes
Were destined; some within a finer mould
She wrought, and tempered with a purer flame:
To these the sire OMNIPOTENT unfolds
The world's harmonious volume, there to read
The transcript of himself.'

I never read these lines, but I feel myself, for the moment, a poet of a far superior order than that to which I really belong."

In a life of LORD BYRON, published a year or two since, I was greatly surprised, and, as a friend of the party, whose memory is aggrieved, not a little offended at the biographer's having given permanence to what, I should hope, was but a mere momentary opinion of Lord Byron, in respect to BLOOMFIELD.

Lord Byron was, doubtless, a captivating poet;

but his critical qualifications were slight. To be so good a man as Robert Bloomfield were a distinction almost enough for any. That he should have pined away the latter years of his life in hopeless poverty is a disgrace to the times, in which he lived ; and England can no longer reproach Scotland with bitterness for the fate of Burns. A more innocent, mild, and unassuming man never adorned the humble sphere in which he moved. His modesty and merit, therefore, ought to have protected his memory from the cold and heartless sneer of worthless vanity. Lord Byron might have learnt many noble lessons of conduct from the poet, he presumed to despise ; since that poet—born in one of the humblest stations in civilized society—never wrote one word, and probably never entertained one thought, that might not be written in letters of gold.

Bloomfield was of mean parentage ; and so was Akenside. The lower the rank, the greater the merit. Though many persons affect to despise pedigree, it is very certain, that no one really does so, who has any distinction of that sort to boast of. It is characteristic of the duke, the peasant, and the savage. But these are not times in which men can be successfully ridiculed for their birth, professions, callings, or trades. The best of sovereigns was a husbandman*. If ridicule must be cast, let it be thrown on vice, folly, insolence, and pretension; but let it not be cast on men, more intrinsically to be admired, than many members of the first families in the kingdom. Had BACON only been a viscount, would he have stood at the head of modern philosophy? Had BYRON only been a baron, he had already fulfilled the purpose for which he lived; and might now sleep—assured of forgetfulness—in the vault of his ancestors.

The subject of Akenside was of the highest class; it could not, therefore, be made a subject for contempt with any one. Can the poetry of Bloomfield? He borrowed nothing from the Greek, the Latin, the French, or the Italian: though some of his coincidences with the Greek poets are particularly remarkable. Nature only was his book; hence his PASTORALS are superior to any others in the language; and his poem, descriptive of a Farmer's life, is, perhaps, second only to Virgil's Georgics.

> " Fret not thyself, thou glittering child of pride,
>   That a poor Villager inspires my strain;
>   With thee let Pageantry and Power abide;
>   The gentle Muses haunt the sylvan reign;

---

* Piastus, King of Poland.

Where through wild groves at eve the lonely swain
Enraptur'd roams, to gaze on Nature's charms.
They hate the sensual, and scorn the vain ;
The parasite their influence never warms ;
Nor him, whose sordid soul the love of gold alarms."

Akenside had now advanced to the 49th year of his age.   He was in the zenith, as it were, of intellectual life ; in the enjoyment of an agreeable, though not an extensive practice ; celebrated as a poet ; blessed with many friends, and one not to be surpassed ; and in connexion with all which, he was blessed beyond the ordinary race of mortals, in the power of commanding true happiness in the enjoyment of an elegant mind, a benevolent heart, and views, far from being too ambitious for his peace.

In the midst of all this, he was suddenly seized with a putrid sore throat, which terminated in his death on the 23d of June, 1770.   He died in Bloomsbury-square, and was buried in St. James's church.   Mr. Dyson administered to his effects, and became possessor of his books, furniture, MSS., and other property, as Akenside had directed, previous to his death.

Though Akenside did not attach himself to any of his brother-poets, he had a long list of friends ; amongst whom, in addition to those already mentioned, were Sir Francis Drake, Bart., the Earl of Huntingdon, Dr. Markham, Lord North, Dr. Reeve, Sir John Hawkins, Mr. Cracherode, Dr. Wharton, and Dr. Birch.

" He was a most unprejudiced and candid estimater of contemporary poets," says Mr. Hardinge; " for which I admired him the more on account of its amiable singularity." The opinion of his judgment by friends may be judged of by the following letter from Dr. Birch to Mr. Wray. " You know the eagerness of our curiosity here for what occurs in the republic of letters ; for which reason you will furnish yourself, before your journey, with such new productions as may deserve our perusal, or such an account of them as may be equivalent to the works themselves. Vaillant may probably supply you with some *Journaux des Sçavans,* imported within this month or six weeks. But we do not exact from you the purchase of the ' MEMOIRS OF LORD BOLINGBROKE,' which, I judge, from Dr. AKENSIDE's account of the book, not to be worth it ; though, if any friend of yours has hazarded four shillings for it, and is willing to spare it, for a few days, we shall not be disinclined to see what the Apologist can say for a character so exceptionable *."

* Nichols' Illust. iv. 534.

The features of Akenside were expressive and manly in a very high degree; but his complexion was pale, and his deportment solemn. He dressed, too, in a very precise manner, and wore a powdered wig in stiff curl. In respect to disposition, he is said to have been irritable, and to have had little restraint upon his temper before strangers; with whom he was precise and ceremonious, stiff, and occasionally sententious and dictatorial.

He had no taste for humour; had little patience in respect to jests; and having no wit himself, could ill brook the coarse wit of others; and was, moreover, of Lord Waldegrave's opinion, that a true gentleman never jests. Yet he was himself a satirist, and had no mean talent that way, as many of his poems testify. But in the following passage, it is impossible, that he could have alluded to Pope, as some have asserted, and many have believed.

> " Thee, too, facetious *Momion !* wandering here;
> Thee, dreaded censor ! oft I have beheld,
> Bewilder'd unawares : alas ! too long
> Flush'd with thy comic triumphs, and the spoils
> Of sly derision !—till on every side,
> Hurling thy random bolts, offended Truth
> Assign'd thee here thy station, with the slaves
> Of Folly.—Thy *once* formidable name
> Shall grace her humble records, and be heard,

In scoffs and mockery, bandied from the lips
Of all the vengeful brotherhood around ;
So *oft* the patient victims of thy scorn."

P. 7, B. III. l. 179.

Some, I say, have imagined the poet to have, in this passage, alluded to Pope ; and Mrs. Barbauld, after admitting its probability, goes on to observe —" Surely, no man of just moral taste can reflect without regret, that a capital work of one of our best poets, composed in the height of his reputation, and during the perfection of all his powers, should have no other end, than to gratify the spleen of an offended author, and to record the petty warfare of rival wits."

These observations are, certainly, just :—but the fact is, Akenside could not allude to Pope in this passage ; for it is evident that the poet had *seen* the person whom he satirizes.

" Thee, dreaded censor ! oft *I have beheld*
Bewilder'd unawares : alas ! too long
Flush'd with thy comic triumphs, and the spoils
Of sly derision."

Now, few things are more certain, than that Akenside never visited London, till his arrival from Leyden ; and that he offered his poem to Dodsley almost immediately after is equally certain. It

is very unlikely, that he should have seen Pope
during the time, in which his poem was printing: but even if he had done so, it must have
been with complacency (and then not " often");
since Pope had desired Dodsley to make him no
mean offer, as he was " no every day writer." The
passage, there can be little doubt, refers to some
pompous, facetious, and censorious blockhead,
whom Akenside had been in the habit of seeing at
Newcastle, at Edinburgh, or at Leyden.

The Hon. GEORGE HARDINGE says in his letter
to Mr. Nichols, that Akenside's " great powers,
besides the talent for poetry, were, those of eloquent
reasoning, historical knowledge, and philosophical
taste, enlivened by the happiest and most brilliant
allusions."   " He had, too, a most astonishing memory, and a most luminous application of it."

SIR JOHN HAWKINS says of his conversation,
that it was of the most delightful kind; learned,
instructive, and without any affectation of wit;
cheerful and highly entertaining :—and he gives an
account of a dinner party, which he enjoyed with
him, Mr. Dyson, and another friend, at Putney;
when the poet, surrounded by his friends, and enjoying their society in the enlivening sunshine of a
summer's day, seemed to feel a joy, that he lived;

and in consequence poured out his gratulations and thanksgiving to the great Dispenser of all felicity in words, which Plato himself might have uttered on a similar occasion.

Yet he was not always agreeable in conversation. He had a high sense of his own merits; and when persons of an inferior cast presumed upon their ignorance, or want of good-breeding, to intrude their observations too unceremoniously, Akenside seldom denied himself the satisfaction of chastising their presumption, by the adoption of a manner, perhaps too severe, satirical, and splenetic. But in the society of those mild and gentle spirits, who admired his genius, and respected his virtues, he was kindness itself. His language flowed chastely, gracefully, and eloquently; and his varied knowledge, argumentative reasonings, and nice distinctions; his fine appreciation of philosophical allusions, and keen relish for the beauties of the creation, would display themselves in pure and copious streams of eloquence, never, perhaps, surpassed by the greatest masters of social life, the world ever knew.

His memory was at once discriminative and comprehensive. He retained all the riches of art, science, and history, legislation, poetry, and philosophy; and these he would draw out and embody to suit the occasion, required, in a manner, not more wonderful to those, who were partially informed, than delightful to those, who could follow his track, and continue with him to the end.

Yet he is said to have, in general, wanted gaiety of heart in society. He was naturally of a cheerful temper; but his cheerfulness was accompanied by a mellowness of feeling, which sometimes relapsed into melancholy. Not that corrosive melancholy, however, which unstrings the mind and renders it incapable of life and action; but of that sweet and delightful nature, which DYER has so beautifully characterized in his " Ruins of Rome."

——————— " There is a mood
(I sing not to the vacant or the young),
There is a kindly mood of melancholy,
That wings the soul, and points her to the skies."

NOTES, &c.

NOTES, &c.

" Soon after the publication of the Pleasures of Imagination, Akenside," says Mr. Dyson, " became conscious that it wanted revision and correction: but so quick was the demand for successive editions, that in any of the intervals to have completed the whole of his corrections was impossible. He chose, therefore, to continue reprinting it without any corrections or improvements, until he should be able at once to give them to the public complete; and with this view he went on, for several years, to review and correct his poem at leisure, till at length he found the task grow so much upon his hands, that, despairing ever being able to execute it to his own satisfaction, he abandoned the purpose of correcting, and resolved to write the poem over anew, upon a somewhat different and enlarged plan; and in the execution of this design, he had made a considerable progress." He printed the first and second books for his own private use; and transcribed a considerable portion of the third book, in order to its being printed in the same manner: "and to these," continues Mr. Dyson, "he added the introduction to a subsequent book, which in MS. is called the fourth, and which appears to have been composed at the time, when the author intended to comprise the whole in four books; but as he afterwards determined to distribute the poem into more books, might, perhaps, more properly be called the last book. This," continues Mr. Dyson, "is all that is executed of the new work; which, although it appeared to the editor too valuable, even in its imperfect state, to be withholden from the public, yet (he conceives) takes in by much too small a part of the original poem to supply its place, and to supersede the republication of it."

Besides this, Akenside left behind him a copy of the original poem with marginal alterations, which came into the possession of the late Mr. Pinkerton, who published them in a collection of letters on various subjects, under the name of Robert Heron.

What Akenside proposed in the second poem is thus laid down by himself in the general argument.

"The Pleasures of the Imagination proceed either from natural objects; as *from a flourishing grove, a clear and murmuring fountain, a calm sea by moon-*

light;—or, from works of art, such as a noble edifice, a musical tune, a statue, a picture, a poem.

" In treating of these pleasures, we must begin with the former class; they being original to the other; and nothing more being necessary, in order to explain them, than a view of our natural inclination towards greatness and beauty, and of those appearances, in the world around us, to which that inclination is adapted *.

" But the pleasures, which we receive from the *elegant arts, from music, sculpture, painting, and poetry,* are much more varied and complicated.

" In them (besides GREATNESS and BEAUTY, or forms proper to the imagination) we find interwoven frequent representations *of truth, of virtue and of vice, of circumstances, proper to move us with laughter, or to excite in us pity, fear, and the other passions* †.

" With the above-mentioned causes of pleasure, which are universal in the course of human life, and appertain to our higher faculties, many others do generally occur, more limited in their operation, or of an inferior origin: such are *the novelty of objects, the association of ideas, affections of the bodily senses, influence of education, national habits, and the like* ‡.

---

* " This is the subject of the first book."

† " These moral and intellectual objects are described in the second book; to which the third properly belongs as an episode, though too large to have been included in it."

‡ " To illustrate these, and from the whole to determine the character of a perfect taste, is the argument of the fourth book."

" Hitherto the Pleasures of the Imagination belong to the human species in general.   But there are certain particular men, whose imagination *is endowed with powers, and susceptible of pleasures, which the generality of mankind never participate.*   These are the MEN of GENIUS, destined by nature, to excel in one or other of the arts, already mentioned.

" It is proposed, therefore, in the last place, to delineate that genius, which, in some degree, appears common to them all ; yet with a more particular consideration of POETRY; inasmuch as poetry is the *most extensive of those arts, the most philosophical, and the most useful."*

That Pope injured the Dunciad, by extending it from three books to four, is universally admitted ; and that Akenside's second poem is inferior to the first, is, I believe, as universally conceded.   It is dangerous for an author to be too difficult to please, and too diffident of himself.   Founded on the papers of Addison in the Spectator, bearing the same title; and many of its passages being associated with the works of Shaftesbury and Hutcheson, there may be some question as to whether Akenside can be strictly styled an original writer ; yet, I think, that praise cannot justly be denied to him ; since in his poem, as an elegant critic has observed with great propriety, he has united the grace of Virgil, the colouring of

Milton, and the incidental expression of Shakespeare, to paint the finest features of the human
mind, and the most lovely forms of true morality and
religion.

His periods are, however, frequently too long;
many of his images are too splendid to be clearly
observed; there is, occasionally, a redundancy of
words; and Johnson criticises with his accustomed judgment, when he says, that the reader
wanders through the gay diffusion, sometimes
amazed, and sometimes delighted; that the sense is
carried on through a long intertexture of complicated clauses; and that his images are displayed
with such luxuriance of expression, that they are
lost under a superfluity of dress.

The second poem has more solidity than the first;
but less power. It is more correct and severe; but
less brilliant, less touching, less enchanting; and the
imagination is seldom so agreeably carried

" Beyond the visible diurnal sphere."

" Had Akenside completed his plan," says Dr.
Aikin, " his poem would have lost as much in
poetry as it would have gained in philosophy."
" If his genius," says Mrs. Barbauld, " is to
be estimated from this poem, it will be found to be

lofty and elegant, chaste, correct, and classical; not marked with strong traits of originality, not ardent, nor exuberant. His enthusiasm was rather of that kind, which is kindled by reading, and imbibing the spirit of authors, than by contemplating at first hand the works of nature. As a versifier, Akenside is allowed to stand amongst those, who have given the most finished models of blank verse. His periods are long, but harmonious; the cadences full of grace; and the measure is supported with uniform dignity. His Muse possessed the *mien erect,* and high commanding gait We shall scarcely find a low or trivial expression introduced, a careless and unfinished line permitted to stand. His stateliness, however, is somewhat allied to stiffness. His verse is sometimes feeble, through too rich a redundancy of ornament; and sometimes laboured into a degree of obscurity, from too anxious a desire of avoiding natural and simple expressions."

Such is the appreciation of Mrs. Barbauld; and, as a kindred specimen of criticism, we may append the opinion of a French critic.

" *Le poëme des Plaisirs de l'Imagination, qui a été accueilli avec enthousiasme dans son origine, est encore regardé comme un des plus beaux monuments de la poésie Anglaise; il est cependant moins lu*

*qu'il n'est admiré. Il est écrit en vers blancs, comme
le poëme de Milton ; et Akenside a peut-être mieux
connu que Milton même l'harmonie propre à ce genre
de poésie. Le style est digne du sujet ; le ton en est
élevé, la couleur brillante, et la diction très-figurée ;
mais les idées trop metaphysiques qui y dominent,
l'emploi trop fréquent des termes abstraits, et
l'abus des metaphores repandent sur tout l'ouvrage
une certaine obscurité que fatigue l'esprit."*

In the first instance, the poem, as before observed,
is founded on Addison's celebrated papers in the
Spectator, illustrative of the same subject ; and certain passages in Lord Shaftesbury's Characteristics,
and Hutcheson's Inquiry into the Original of our
Ideas of Beauty and Virtue. Some thoughts are,
also, acknowledged to have been taken from Plato
and Aristotle ; one from Longinus ; and several
from the *De Rerum Natura* of Lucretius.

BOOK THE FIRST.

——————— " Attend, ye powers
Of *musical* delight !"

B. I. l. 6.

Whether Akenside ever attached himself to any musical instrument does not appear.   But that he was passionately devoted to music, as a hearer, there can be little doubt.   The love of sweet sounds is almost native to the poetical character.   But we have a still better evidence to offer ; and that is a note, appended to the original edition of his great poem, which has,—wherefore I am at a loss to conjecture,—been omitted in most of the subsequent editions.

" The word *musical* is here taken in its original and most extensive import ; comprehending as well the pleasures, we receive from the beauty or magnificence of *natural* objects, as those which arise from poetry, painting, music, or any other of the elegant and imaginative arts.   In which sense, it has already been used in our language, by writers of unquestionable authority."

From this note it appears, that Akenside attached the idea of music to every thing, that was agreeable to him, whether in Nature or in Art.

———————— " But the love
Of Nature and the Muses bid explore,
Through secret paths, erewhile untrod of man,
The fair poetic region,—to detect
Untasted springs, to drink inspiring draughts,
And shade my temples with unfading flowers,
Cull'd from the laureate vale's profound recess,
Where never poet gain'd a wreath before."

I. 48.

Partly from an exquisite passage in Lucretius :—

" Nunc age, quod super est, cognosce, et clarius audi :
Nec me animi fallit, quam sit obscura ; sed acri
Percussit thyrso laudis spes magna meum cor,
Et simul incussit suavem mî in pectus amorem
Musarum : quo nunc instinctus, mente vigenti
Avia Pieridum peragro loca, nullius ante
Trita solo : juvat integros adcedere funteis,
Atque haurire ; juvatque novos decerpere flores,
Insignemque meo capiti petere inde coronam,
Unde prius nulli velarint tempora Musæ."

De Rerum Natura, Lib. I. v. 920.

Virgil, too :

" Nec sum animi dubius, verbis ea vincere magnum
Quam sit, et angustis hunc addere rebus honorem.
Sed me Parnassi deserta per ardua dulcis
Raptat Amor ; juvat ire jugis, qua nulla priorum
Castaliam molli devertitur orbita clivo."

Georg. III. 289.

——————— " Ere the radiant sun
Sprang from the east, or mid the vault of night
The moon suspended her serener lamp;
Ere mountains, woods, or streams adorn'd the globe,
Or wisdom taught the sons of men her lore;
Then lived the ALMIGHTY ONE."   *I. l.* 59.

This fine passage seems to have been conceived from a few lines in a poem, containing an
insufferable degree of bombast with some portion,
and more imitation, of Miltonic fire.   It is entitled
the LAST DAY; written by J. BULKELEY, Esq. of
Clare Hall, Cambridge, and published in 1720.

" Ere TITAN learn'd to shower his golden streams,
  Ere clouds adorn'd the air, or stars the void,
  Nature dropp'd dormant, in the bosom lost
  Of savage chaos ———————
  Rude rocks, misshapen hills, and globes unform'd,
  Then rose the ALMIGHTY," &c.

Probably Akenside had read Georgius:——

" Unus perfectus Deus est, qui cuncta creavit,
  Cuncta fovens, atque ipse fovens super omnia in se;
  Quis capitur mente tantum, qui mente videtur;"
&c. &c.
                    FRANC. GEORG. *in Lib. de Hermo de Mund.**

---

* Beauties and Sublimities of Nature, vol. iv. p. 163.

Thus Milton :—

—————— " Before the sun,
Before the heavens thou wert; and at the voice
Of God, as with a mantle, didst invest
The rising world of waters, dark and deep,
Won from the dark and formless infinite."

Thus Maximus Tyrius:—" *God is the Father
and Creator of every thing, that exists ; before the
sun he is ; and before the heavens existed, to him a
being.*"

In Ovid, we read :—

" Ante mare et tellus, et, quod legit omnia, cœlum,
  Unus erat toto Naturæ vultus," &c.

Met. I. l. 5.

In the Psalms, xl. 2.—" *Before the mountains
were brought forth, or ever thou hadst formed the
earth and the worlds, even from everlasting to
everlasting thou art God.*"

In the laws of Menu :—" *This universe existed
only in the first divine idea, yet unexpanded,* as if
involved in darkness, and as if it were wholly im-
mersed in sleep. Then the self-existing power
appeared expanding his idea," &c.

Petrarch has a very extravagant idea:—" The
beauty of Laura existed in the conception of the
Divinity, before the creation of the universe."

—————— " From the first
Of days, on them his love divine he fix'd—
His admiration; till in time complete
What he admired and loved, his vital *smile*
Unfolded into being."——————   *I. l.* 70.

There is a singular coincidence of thought between this fine passage, and a beautiful one in a Hindoo hymn to " the Spirit of God," translated by Sir Wm. Jones.   There is, also, a similar idea in a fragment of Orpheus, quoted by Proclus; and another in the Edda of Sæmund.

—————— " With wise intent,
The hand of Nature on peculiar minds
Imprints a different bias; and to each
Decrees its province in the common toil."
                                        B. I. v. 82.

Thus Lucretius:

—————— " Quam vis doctrina politos
Constituat pariter quosdam, tamen illa relinquit
Natura quoiusque animi vestigia prima."
                            De Rer. Nat. III. 308.

" For as old MEMNON's image, long renown'd
   By fabling Nilus, to the quivering touch
   Of TITAN's ray, with each repulsive string
   Consenting, sounded through the warbling air
   Unbidden strains;—e'en so did Nature's hand,
   To certain species of external things,
   Attune the finer organs of the mind."
                                        I. l. 109.

Akenside appears to have caught this idea from a passage in one of Moliere's comedies: "*Mademoiselle, ne plus, ne moins que la statue de Memnon rendoit un son harmonieux lorsqu'elle venoit à être éclairée des rayons du soleil ; tout de même me sens-je animé d'un doux transport à l'apparition du soleil de vos beautés.*"

LE MALADE IMAGINAIRE, A. II. S. 5.

There is, also, a passage, allied to this, in Lope de Vega's heroic poem of "*La Hermosura de Angelica :*"

" Que coma con la musica se haze,
Concorde son," &c. &c. *

Porphyry has a beautiful idea. The original is not at hand ; but the sense stands thus :—" In our sensations, the soul moves, as if embodied Harmony itself should play upon an instrument, and smartly touch the well-tuned strings ; but the body is like that harmony, which dwells in the springs themselves, which have no perception of it."

* Vid. Beauties, Harmonies, and Sublimities of Nature, vol. iv. p. 161.

In the MS. corrected copy the reading stands thus:

" As Memnon's marble form, renown'd of old
  By fabling Nilus, at the potent touch
  Of morning utter'd from its inmost frame
  Unbidden music ; so hath Nature's hand
  To certain species of external things
  Attuned the finer organs of the mind.
  So the glad impulse of congenial powers,
  Or of sweet sound, or fair proportion'd form,
  The grace of motion, or the pomp of light,
  Shoots through Imagination's tender frame ;
  Through every naked nerve ; till all the soul
  To that harmonious movement now resigns
  Her functions.   Then the inexpressive strain
  Diffuseth its enchantment.   Fancy dreams,
  Rapt into high discourse with sainted bards ;
  And, wandering through Elysium, fancy dreams
  Of mystic fountains, and inspiring groves ;
  Fountains, the haunt of ORPHEUS ; happy groves,
  Where MILTON dwells.   The intellectual power
  Bends from his solemn throne a wondering ear
  And smiles :—The Passions to divine repose
  Persuaded yield ; and Love and Joy alone
  Are waking ; Love and Joy, such as await
  An angel's meditation."

It is, perhaps, not too much to say, that this is
the finest and most splendid passage in the whole
range of didactic poetry.

In respect to the statue, Akenside, in the original
edition, had appended the following note :—

" The statue of Memnon, so famous in antiquity, stood in the temple of Serapis at Thebes, one of the great cities of old Egypt. It was of a very hard, iron-like substance *; and, according to Juvenal, held in its hand a lyre, which, being touched by the sun-beams, emitted a distinct and agreeable sound. Tacitus mentions it as one of the principal curiosities, which Germanicus took notice of, in his journey through Egypt; and Strabo † affirms, that he, with many others, heard it."

The first seven lines, as originally written, are thus rendered by Mazza :

" Come l'Imago di MEMNON, cui nome
    Eterno die la favolosa Egitto,
    Agli urti primi del Titanio raggio
    Prouta movea l'obbedienti corde,
    Che, tremolando, lo spontaneo suono
    Per entro il gorgheggiante aere spandeano,
    Così Natura ancor gli esterni oggetti
    A' nostri più sottili organi accorda."

---

* Philostratus says it was of black marble. In Vit. Apol. vi. c. 4.

† It is mentioned, also, by Pliny (*Nat. Hist.* vii. c. 56.), Pausanias, and Juvenal:

" Dimidis magicæ resonant ubi Memnone Chordæ."

——————— " Then the inexpressive strain," &c.
B. I. l. **124.**

" When we want to render an object beautiful or
magnificent," says Blair, " we borrow images from
all the most beautiful or splendid scenes of nature;
we thereby, naturally, throw a lustre over our object;
we enliven the reader's mind ; and dispose him to go
along with us, in the gay and pleasing impressions,
which we give him of the subject. This effect of
figures is happily touched in the following lines of
Akenside, and illustrated by a very sublime figure :

———————' Then the inexpressive strain
Diffuses its enchantment,' " &c.

———————" O, attend,
Whoe'er thou art," &c.   *I. l.* **132.**

This passage stands differently in the MS. :

——————— ——" O ! attend,
Whoe'er thou art, whom these delights can touch,
Whom *Nature's aspect, Nature's simplest garb,*
Can thus command ; O ! listen to my song,
And I will guide thee to her *blissful* walks,
And teach thy solitude her voice to hear,
And point her *gracious* features to thy view."
Second Poem.

——————— ——" O ! attend,
Whoe'er thou art, whom these delights can *move,*

Whose candid bosom this primæval love
Of Nature warms; O! listen to my song,
And I will guide thee to her *holiest* walks,
And teach her solitude thy voice to hear,
And point her *awful* features to thy view."

MS.

" The powers of Fancy, her delighted sons
   To THREE illustrious orders have referr'd,
   Three sister Graces, whom the painter's hand,
   The poet's tongue, confesses; the *sublime,*
   The *wonderful,* the *fair.*"

B. I. 142.

This division is from ADDISON: the poet, however, in his second poem, reduces the number from three to two.

" In TWO illustrious orders comprehend
   Self-taught.   From him, whose rustic toil, the lark
   Cheers warbling,—to the bard, whose daring thoughts
   Range the full orb of being, still the form
   Which fancy worships, or SUBLIME or FAIR,
   Her votaries proclaim."

B. I. 183.

In the MS. corrected copy:

———" To the bard, *whose mighty mind*
   Grasps the full orb of being; still the form
   Which fancy worships, or sublime or fair,
   Their eager tongues proclaim."

These alterations it is highly important to note.

R

They are delightful evidences of the mechanism of a poet's mind; than which nothing, perhaps, is more agreeable to the imagination in the whole laboratory of mental exercise.

———————

"Say, why was man so eminently raised
   Amid the vast creation——"

down to

" Who that from Alpine heights, his labouring eye
  Shoots round the wide horizon to survey
  Nilus, or Ganges, rolling his bright wave,
  Through mountains, plains, through empires black with
    shade,
  And continents of sand, will turn his gaze
  To mark the windings of a scanty rill,
  That murmurs at his feet?"
                      B. I. v. 151—183.

These admirable lines are founded on a passage in Longinus*; which the poet acknowledges and translates †.

* De Sub. Sect. xxxv.
† " Those god-like geniuses were well assured, that Nature had not intended man for a low spirited or ignoble being; but bringing us into life, and in the midst of this wide universe, as before a multitude assembled at some heroic solemnity, that we might be spectators of all her magnificence, and candidates high in emulation for the prize of glory. She has, therefore, implanted in our souls an inextinguishable love of every thing great and exalted, of every thing which appears divine beyond our comprehension. Whence it comes

---

" Who that from Alpine heights, &c.?"

B. I. l. 177.

Dr. Johnson objects to the epithet *Alpine*. His note is a curious instance of the facility, with which

to pass, that even the whole world is not an object, sufficient for the depth and rapidity of human imagination, which often sallies forth beyond the limits of all that surrounds us. Let any man cast his eye through the whole circle of our existence, and consider how especially it abounds in excellent and grand objects, he will soon acknowledge for what enjoyments and pursuits we were destined. Thus by the very propensity of nature we are led to admire, not little springs or shallow rivulets, however clear and delicious, but the Nile, the Rhine, the Danube, and, much more than all, the ocean *."

---

* It must be confessed, that this version is greatly inferior to that of Smith : which forms, perhaps, the most sublime passage in the whole extension of translated prose. It has, in fact, almost every quality, by which excellence in the higher departments of language can be recognised.

" Nature never designed Man to be a grovelling and ungenerous animal : but brought him into life, and placed him in the world, as in a crowded theatre, not to be an idle spectator, but spurned on by an eager thirst of excelling, ardently to contend in the pursuit of glory. For this purpose, she implanted in his soul an invincible love of grandeur, and a constant emulation of whatever seems to approach nearer to divinity than himself. Hence it is, that the whole universe is not sufficient for the extensive reach and piercing specula-

even eminent minds can fall into the errors, they are ambitious of correcting.

" The sense of his words is strained," says Johnson, " when he views Ganges from *Alpine* heights; that is, from mountains like the Alps; and the pedant surely intrudes (but when was blank verse without pedantry?) when he tells us how planets *absolve* the stated round of time." Surely, this is in itself an instance of true pedantry. Akenside, however, seems himself to have wavered, in respect to the propriety of using this finely descriptive epithet; for in the second poem, he writes " aerial;" and in his marginal notes " mid-air."

———— " Now, amazed, she views
The empyreal waste, where happy spirits hold,
Beyond the concave heaven, their calm abode."

I. v. 201.

tion of the human understanding.   It passes the bounds of the material world, and launches forth at pleasure into endless space.   Let any one take an exact survey of life, which, in its every sense, is conspicuous on account of excellence, grandeur, and beauty; and he will soon discern for what noble ends we were born.   Thus the impulse of nature inclines us to admire, not a little, clear, transparent rivulet, that administers to our necessities; but the Nile, the Isther, the Rhine, and still more the ocean."

The passage, quoted from Leibnitz, in all the editions of Akenside, is incorrect and incomplete. It stands thus in the last Paris edition : — " *D'ailleurs, comme il n'y a nulle raison qui porte à croire qu'il y a des étoiles par tout, ne se peut-il point qu'il y ait un grand espace au dela de la region des étoiles ? Que ce soit le ciel empyrée, ou non, toûjours cet espace immense, qui environne tout cette region, pourra être rempli de bonheur et de gloire. Il pourra être conçu comme l'ocean, où se rendent les fleuves de toutes les creatures bien heureuses, quand elles seront venues à leur perfection dans le systeme des étoiles.*"—LEIBNITZ *dans la Theodicée. Part I. Sect.* 19.

Akenside seems, also, to have remembered two lines in Lucretius : —

" Omnis enim per se divôm natura, necesse est,
Immortali ævo summâ cum pace fruatur."
De Rerum Natura, II. 645.

Mr. Murphy, in a poetical epistle to Dr. Johnson, after enumerating several examples of " wealthy genius, pining midst its store," joins GRAY and AKENSIDE after the following manner :

" E'en GRAY, unwilling, strikes his living lyre,
And wishes, not content, for Pindar's fire :

And that sweet bard, who to our fancy brings
' *The gayest, happiest attitude of things,*'
His raptured verse can throw, neglected, by,
And to Lucretius lift a reverend eye."

———

———— " Fields of radiance, whose unfading light
Has travell'd the profound six thousand years,
Nor yet arrives in sight of mortal things."   *B. I.* 204.

" Est igitur natura loci, spatiumque profundi,
Quod neque clara suo percurrere lumina cursu
Perpetuo possint ævi labentia tractu;
Nec prorsum facere, ut restet minus ire, meando;
Usque adeo passim patet ingens copia rebus,
Finibus exemptis, in cunctas undique parteis."
                    De Rerum Natura, Lib. I. v. 1001.

" It was a notion of the great Huygens," says
Akenside, " that there may be stars at such a distance from our solar system, as that their light
shall not have had time to reach us, even from the
creation of the world to this day."

Light—which PLATO figuratively calls *the shadow of the divinity*—is about eight minutes and a
half coming to our globe from the sun. From a
knowledge of this velocity, it is proved that the
rays of light, which we receive from Sirius, are six
years and four and a half months traversing the
space between us. But when we consider the
distance of some of the nebulæ, it is calculated that
the light, we receive from them, cannot be less than

two millions of years upon its journey! Those
nebulæ must, therefore, have existed, at the least,
two millions of years before their light could first
reach the hemisphere of the earth; while we,—
presumptuous as we are!—have power to prove an
existence of little more than the momentary span
of four thousand nine hundred and five years.

When the eye traverses the universe, the Sun,
and all its accompaniments, sink into comparative
insignificance! When we pierce into the depth
of space, and find, that the whole of what is called
the GALAXY, with all the scattered stars, are to be
considered as forming only one vast *nebula*, to
which our solar system also belongs;—when we
consider, that the distance of one of the stars
in Lyra is from the earth more than twenty
billions of miles; and that its diameter cannot be
less than three-fourths of the size of the entire solar
system, circumscribed as it is to our vision by the
last satellite of URANUS*;—that not less than two

* As the satellites of URANUS move in orbits, perpendicu-
lar to the plane of the Ecliptic, and in a retrograde direction,
contrary to the analogy of all other secondaries, as well as
primaries, they appear to justify a supposition, *that they indicate the approach, if not the actual beginning of another
province of the Solar Empire; of which they are the heralds
and connecting links.*
Some inconvenience having arisen from the circumstance

thousand five hundred nebulæ have been already
traced in the firmament ;—and that the rapidity

of the satellites of SATURN having been numbered, not in
the order of distance, but of discovery; and the names,
given to those of Jupiter by the illustrious Galileo, Simon
Marius, and Baptista Hodierna, having fallen into disuse; I
took the liberty, a short time since, of proposing *another no-
menclature, more in consonance with that, already established
for the larger Planets.* The use and propriety of this nomen-
clature having been conceded by several eminent persons,
perhaps the reader will excuse me for endeavouring to acquire
for it a still more extended consideration.

Satellites of Jupiter.

First in the order of distance . . . Hebe.
Second . . . . Astræa.
Third . . . . Flora.
Fourth . . . . Pomona.

Satellites of Saturn.

First in the order of distance . . . Cybele.
Second . . . . Thetis.
Third . . . . Doris.
Fourth . . . . Hygeia.
Fifth . . . . Echo.
Sixth . . . . Psyche.
Seventh . . . . Fortuna.

Satellites of Uranus (Herschel).

First in the order of distance . . . Urania.
Second . . . . Calliope.
Third . . . . Clio.
Fourth . . . . Melpomene.
Fifth . . . . Thalia.
Sixth . . . . Erato.

of motion, by which stars are upheld in their relative positions, is so great, that the revolutions of two (apparently forming one), in the constellation of Ursa Major, round their centre of gravity, may be traced from month to month;— when we contemplate, I say, the number, the magnitude, the vastness of distance, the velocity and regularity of motion; system beyond system, and nebula beyond nebula; presenting to the imagination, at every step, new forms of life and new orders of intelligence,—the mind becomes impressed with a sublimity of admiration, so full and so entire, that it is with no surprise we afterwards come to the conclusion, that those, who thus with the works of the Deity " hold converse," must, as a natural result, more intimately, though perhaps more silently, than any other men,

> ———— " Act upon his plan,
> And form to his the relish of their souls."

The finest and most sublime poetical conception, that has yet entered into the mind of man, appears to be that, which pictures innumerable suns, rising out of chaos; and, in rising, throwing out their planets; those planets sending out their satellites; all moving with inconceivable rapidity, orb with-

in orb, round some general centre;—these suns,
planets, and satellites sinking periodically into one
general chaos; and thence again issuing forth, im-
pelled by new impulses, to form regenerated worlds;
and so issuing, returning, and re-issuing, at stated
periods, to all eternity! This picture is presented
in the following lines of Darwin, and I know of
nothing that can be pronounced to be its equal,
much less its superior.

" The LOVE DIVINE *, with brooding wings unfurl'd,
  Call from the rude abyss the living world.
  ' *Let there be light !*' exclaim'd the Almighty Lord.
  Astonish'd CHAOS heard the potent word;
  Through all his realms the kindling ether runs,
  And the mass starts into a million suns:

---

* ———— LOVE, the sire of FATE,
      Elder than CHAOS.

                          Hymn to the Naiads, l. 1.

The LOVE, designed in the text, is the ONE SELF-EXISTENT
and *infinite* MIND; whom, if the generality of ancient my-
thologists have not introduced, or truly described, in accounting for the production of the world and its appearances;
yet, to a modern poet, it can be no objection, that he hath
ventured to differ from them in this particular: though, in
other respects, he professeth to imitate their manner and
conform to their opinions. For, in these great points of natural theology, they differ no less remarkably among themselves; and are perpetually confounding the philosophical
relations of things with the traditionary circumstances of
mythic history.—*Akenside.*

Earths round each sun with quick explosions burst,
And second planets issue from the first ;
Bend, as they journey with projectile force,
In bright ellipses, their reluctant course ;
Orbs wheel in orbs, round centres centres roll,
And form, self-balanced, one revolving whole*."

Dr. Olbers, and several other eminent astrono-
mers, have given into the idea, that a large planet
once existed between the orbits of Mars and Jupiter; and that it separated into four parts, forming what are now called the ASTEROIDS.

Much astronomical learning has been called into
action on this subject. It is argued, that BODE's

---

* Who can read the following letter, recently published,
from Dr. Beattie to Garrick, without a smile? It reminds
us of " one *John Milton,*" and of " one *Matthew Prior.*"

" Aberdeen, March 16, 1772.

" I lately received a letter from one, who subscribes himself *E. Darwin, Physician, in Litchfield ;* containing some
objections to an argument, advanced in my essay against
Mr. Hume's doctrine of extended ideas. His manner seems
rather captious; however, I know not how it is, my heart
warms to the man, either because his hand-writing bears
some resemblance to yours, or because he has the honour
to live in the town where you and Johnson were born ; and
therefore I will write to him soon, and I hope to satisfy all
his doubts, which, indeed, seem to arise from his not perfectly understanding either my philosophy, or that which
he himself defends."

law, and the law of Nature, are one ; and that they
both require the existence of such a planet.   If so,
why does not this large body exist?   If it were
wanted in times past, it is wanted in times present;
for all the apprehensions of NEWTON, in regard to
the solar system being susceptible of decay, have
long since been dissipated by LA GRANGE's
discovery—the most splendid in modern times !
—that all the irregularities and inequalities, which
flow from planetary action, are, in reality, so
harmoniously adjusted to the various parts of the
vast machine, as to be, in all cases, constant in
periodical return :—while the labours of La Place
having established the knowledge, that the time of
a planet's revolution, as well as its mean distance
from the sun, are constant properties, it follows, as
a natural result, that all planetary existences are
beyond the reach of accident, and, therefore, for
ever unassailable by time.

Planetary distances are *coincidences*; not *principles*.   If the Asteroids formed, originally, one body,
would not all and each of them present striking and
permanent analogies? What, however, are the facts?
The action of JUNO not only differs from that of
the rest, but from those of all the other known
planets in the solar system.   For when at her

greatest distance from the sun, she is at double the distance she is when at the least; and the part of her orbit, which is bisected by her perihelion, is passed in half the time in which she traverses the one more distant. Then, as to the atmospheres of these planets:—that of VESTA is scarcely observable; that of JUNO is more so; that of PALLAS is still more extended; but Ceres!—her atmospheric substance rises to a height even superior to those of the other planets in the system all combined! Where then is the probability of these bodies having ever formed one? It is even possible, *that CERES and JUNO may constitute connecting links between PLANETS and COMETS:*—a supposition not to be lightly regarded; for it is rendered strikingly probable by the circumstance, that the aphelion of Encke's comet lies at no greater distance from the sun, than the space between the orbit of Jupiter and those of the Asteroids themselves. They all breathe, as it were, in the same hemisphere of the universe.

If the existence of a large planet be necessary, Nature, by causing it to separate; its parts to move in different orbits; and each part to present different phenomena, has violated the most constant and most comprehensive, as well as the most effective and preservative of her laws.

If four planets will answer the purpose of the one, supposed to have burst, as, it appears, they very effectively do, *what difficulty can there be in supposing, that they have existed from the creation and adjustment of the system; as well as Jupiter and Mars and all the other primary and secondary planets?* Why, in fact, should we accuse Nature of having done an act, which is not only unnecessary, but which is in decided opposition to all the laws, by which she can be recognised?

Since the phenomena of gravitation cannot, in any way, be accounted for, either by matter or motion; if philosophers guard themselves against being shackled by the bonds of system, and from being paralysed by the authority even of illustrious names; if they keep themselves free to observe, with unclouded eyes and unbiassed judgments, the varied phenomena, presented to their view, and feelingly awake to every light, that may hereafter emanate from the experience of the ever-teeming laboratory of the human mind, it is not impossible but that the masterly,—nay, the divine,—discovery of LA GRANGE may be found to lead to the propriety of reconsidering the views, that have hitherto been entertained of gravitation. And it is not impossible, that such reconsideration may open the door to the knowledge of *an Agent, hitherto unknown and unthought of, acting with it, though of a nature altogether different from it; and of a subtlety and minute power of application, immeasurably its superior.*

———————

——————— " Witness the neglect
Of all familiar prospects," &c.
B. I. v. 234.

" Principio, cœli clarum purumque colorem,
   Quemque in se cohibent palantia sidera passim,
   Lunamque, et solis præclarâ luce nitorem :
   Omnia quæ nunc si primum mortalibus essent,
   Ex improviso si sint objecta repente ;
   Quid magis hiis rebus poterat mirabile dici,
   Aut minus ante quod auderent fore credere gentes ?
   Nihil, ut opinor ; ita hæc species miranda fuisset :
   Quam, tibi jam nemo, fessus satiate videndi,
   Subspicere in cœli dignatur lucida templa."
        LUCRETIUS; *De Rerum Natura, II. l. 1029.*

A passage in Cowper serves to illustrate this inquiry :

   " What prodigies can power divine perform
      More grand, than it produces, year by year,
      And all in sight of inattentive man ?
      Familiar with th' effect, we slight the cause ;

And, in the constancy of nature's course,
The regular return of genial months,
And renovation of a faded world,
See nought to wonder at.——
All we behold is miracle; but, seen
So duly, all is miracle in vain."

Winter Walk at Noon.

" At every solemn pause the crowd recoil,
Gazing each other speechless and congeal'd
With shivering sighs; till, eager for th' event,
Around the beldame, all erect, they hang,
Each trembling heart with grateful terrors quell'd *.'

B. I. 266.

The original of this is in Addison.

A modern poet has a transcendent passage:

" 'Tis pleasant by the cheerful hearth to hear
Of tempests and the dangers of the deep,
And pause at times, and feel that we are safe:
Then listen to the perilous tale again,
And, with an eager and *suspended soul,*
Woo terror to delight us."

Southey.

There are few passages, even in Shakspeare, superior to this.

* In the MS. notes, there is a direction for the transplanting this passage to Book III. after verse 278.

Sir Walter Scott, also, has a finely characteristic passage in his poem of Rokeby.

" When Christmas logs blaze high and wide,
Such wonders speed the festal tide,
While CURIOSITY and FEAR,
PLEASURE and PAIN, *sit crouching near;*
Till childhood's cheek no longer glows,
And village-maidens lose the rose.
The thrilling interest rises higher,
The circle closes nigh and nigher,
And shuddering glance is cast behind,
*As louder moans the wintry wind *."

---

* Cant. II. St. 10. The astonishing success of this remarkable man may be traced to causes, to a knowledge of which the following passages from Rochefoucault, and his commentator, form an ample key. " *The height of ability,*" says the former, " *consists in a thorough knowledge of the real value of things, and the genius of the age, we live in.*" " *Most of the authors, immortalized by their contemporaries,*" says the latter, " *have been indebted to this knowledge; or else to the luck of living in an age, with whose turn their abilities coincided.*"

An author, of this splendid coincidence, seldom has to wait. Fame haunts him wherever he may go. Those, on the contrary, who look forward, with prophetic eyes, and build on the future enlargement of the human mind, must wait the time, for which they labour.

—— " Brightest progeny of heaven," &c.

B. I. v. 280.

The passage, beginning with this line, and finishing with " Spring's elysian bloom," has been thus translated by Warton.

EX POEMATE DE VOLUPTATIBUS FACULTATIS IMAGINATRICIS.

——" O progenies pulcherrima cæli !
Quo tibi succorum tractu, calamique labore ;
Divinos ducam vultus, cœlestiaque ora?
Unde legam qui, Diva, tuis certare colores
Purpurei possint, discrimina dædala fuci?
Ergo age, Musa, vago cursu per maxima mundi
I spatia ; et quicquid formosi florida tellus,
Quicquid habent maria, et cæli spirabile lumen,
Delibes ; quicquid nitidum natura recondit
*Dives opum variarum** , in amabile, Musa, fideli
Confer opus studio.   Seu liberioribus alis
Vin', comite AUTUMNO, per fortunata volare
Hesperidûm nemora, et dias Atlantidos oras,
Dum quacunque Pater fœcundo pollice lucum
Felicim contingit, opacis gratia ramis
Fit nova, et *auricomo fulsêrunt vimina fœtu†:*
Quâcunque incessit per ditia rura, renident
Undique *maturo subiti livore racemi‡;*
Apricosque recens infecit purpura colles,
Quales occiduo nubes quæ *sole coruscant§.*

---

* Virg. Georg. II. 467.   † Æn. vi. 140.
‡ Hor. Carm. ii. v. 10.   § Georg. i. 233.

Sive errare velis, *rigua convalle**, per umbras
Daphnes dilectas, *Penéus gurgite leni*
Quà fluit†, ostentatque reflexam e flumine Tempe
Purpuream vitreo ; Tempe! quâ, numina sylvis
Nota olim, fauni nymphæque, per aurea prisci
Sæcula Saturni, secreto in margine ripæ
Frondiferæ, socio ducebant Pane choreas
Multiplices.   Ac saltantum *vestigia propter‡.*
Horasque, Zephyrosque almos, udo imbre, videres
Certatim ambrosios rores, et odoriferum thus,
Depluere, Elysioque rubent quicunque colores?"

————————

——————— —————————— " Wilt thou fly,
With laughing Autumn to th' Atlantic isles?"
                                                    I. 287.

  " By these islands, which were, also, called the
Fortunate," says Akenside in a note to the original
edition, " the ancients are now generally supposed
to have meant the *Canaries.*   They were celebrated
by the poets for the mildness and fertility of the
climate; for the gardens of the daughters of Hes-
perus, the brother of Atlas ; and the dragon, which

————————

* Mons. Cath. v. 72.   In obitum Frederici, v. 21.   Virg.
Georg. ii. 485.
  † Hymn. ad Pan. v. 4.   Æn. ii. 781.
  ‡ Lucret. v. 736.

constantly watched their golden fruit, till it was slain
by the Tyrian Hercules."

"Fair Tempe! haunt belov'd of sylvan powers,
  Of nymphs and fauns," &c.

I. v. 299.

This passage is much amplified in the second
poem; not much, perhaps, to the poetical advantage.

From this fountain Warton seems to have caught
a little of his inspiration, while writing the Pleasures
of Melancholy.

——————————— " The laughing scenes
Of purple spring; where all the wanton train
Of smiles and graces seem to lead the dance
In sportive round; while from their hands they shower
Ambrosial blooms and flowers; no longer charm.
TEMPE! no more I court thy balmy breeze:
Adieu, green vales! ye broider'd meads, adieu!"

Pleasures of Melancholy, 21.

We are under great obligations to Akenside: for
had he not written on the Pleasures of the Imagination, we had, possibly, never had " the Pleasures of
Melancholy," " the Pleasures of Memory," or " the
Pleasures of Hope."

——————————— " With these better cares
Th' indulgent mother, conscious how infirm

"Her offspring tread the paths of good and ill,
By this illustrious image, in each kind
Still more illustrious," &c. &c.

I. 357.

Among the MS. notes, this passage stands thus:

" *Now* more illustrious, where the object holds
Its *proper* powers most perfect, she by this
Directs the headlong impulse of desire,
And sanctifies his choice.   The glow of flowers,
Which gild the verdant pasture, the clear track
Of streams delicious to the thirsty soul,
The bloom of *downy* fruitage," &c.

———————————— " Truth and good are one;
That beauty dwells in them, and they in her
With like participation *."

Book I. l. 374.

The poet gives references, also, to several passages
in Shaftesbury.   They are these;—

" I am ready enough to yield," said I, " that there is
no real good beside the enjoyment of beauty."   " And

---

* " Do you imagine," said Socrates to Aristippus, " that
what is good is not beautiful?   Have you not observed, that
these appearances always coincide?   Virtue, for instance, in
the same respect as to which we call good, is ever acknowledged to be beautiful also."—*Xenophon. Memorabil. Socrat.
Lib. III.* c. 8.

I am ready," replied Theocles, " to yield, that there is
no real enjoyment of beauty, beside what is good."—
Charact. II. 422.

" Should not this be still the same case, and hold,
equally as to the mind?   Is there nothing there, which
tends to disturbance and dissolution?   Is there no natural tenour, tone, or order of the passions or affections?
No *beauty* or *deformity* in this *moral* kind? Or, allowing
that there really is, must it not, of consequence, in the
same manner, imply *health* or *sickliness, prosperity* or
disaster?   Will it not be found in this respect above
all, that what is beautiful is *harmonious and proportionable;* what is harmonious and proportionable is TRUE ;
and that what is at once *beautiful and true* is, of consequence, *agreeable and good.*   Where, then, is this
BEAUTY or HARMONY to be found?   How is this SYM-
METRY to be discovered and applied?   Is it any other
art than that of PHILOSOPHY, or the *study of inward
numbers and proportions,* which can exhibit this in life?
If no other; who, then, can possibly have a taste of this
kind, without being beholden to philosophy? Who can
admire the *outward* beauties, and not recur instantly to
the *inward,* which are the most real and essential, the
most naturally affecting, and of the highest pleasure, as
well as profit and advantage."—Vol. iii. 181, 3, 4, 5.

For Shaftesbury's opinions, generally, on this
subject, see Moral Beauty, II. 409.   Beauty
of Sentiments, Character of Mind, I. 136, 207;

III. 303.   That Beauty is Truth, I. 142; III. 180,
&c.   Beauty of Virtue, I. 315.   Scale of Beauty,
III. 218.   How attractive and enchanting, III.
216, 218.   Its extent, II. 211, 212, 213.

It is scarcely possible to read the passages, here
referred to, without recurring to Gray's poem, *De
Principiis cogitandi.*

> —————— —————— " Sapientia dia
> Hinc roseum accendit lumen, vultuque sereno
> Humanas aperit mentes, nova gaudia monstrans,
> Deformesque fugat curas, vanosque timores;
> Scilicet et rerum crescit pulcherrima virtus."

Will the reader excuse me for introducing in this
place a passage from the Harmonies of Nature?   It
belongs expressly to the subject.

" Every object, which awakens pleasure in the mind,
is beautiful; since it produces the sensation of pleasure.
Whatever excites agreeable emotion, therefore, possesses
some intrinsic quality of beauty.   Hence the term beauty
may be applied to every thing, which gives pleasure to
the mind; from a woman to a problem; from a planet
to a tree or a flower.   Hence arises the intimate connexion between beauty and virtue.

" In the spirit of this doctrine, WIELAND, the celebrated German poet, has written a dialogue, conceived
in the manner, and executed with much of the sweet-
ness and delicacy of Plato.   He imagines SOCRATES to
surprise TIMOCLEA, a captivating Athenian virgin, at

her toilette; dressed for a solemn festival in honour of Diana; attired in all the beauty of Nature and all the luxuriance of art. His surprising her in this manner gives rise to a dialogue, in which the subject of real and apparent BEAUTY is philosophically discussed. The arguments are summed up by TIMOCLEA, at the end of the discourse, in which she declares herself a convert to that fine moral doctrine, which teaches, *that nothing is beautiful, which is not good; and nothing good, but what is, at the same time, intrinsically beautiful.*"

" Unless the IMAGINATION be excited, as Mr. Alison observes *, the emotions of beauty and sublimity are unfelt. Hence, whatever increases the powers of that faculty, increases those emotions in like proportion; and no objects or qualities being felt, either as beautiful or sublime, but such as are productive of some simple emotion, no composition of objects, or qualities, produce emotions of taste, in which that unity is not preserved."

———

———— " Not let the gleam
Of youthful hope," &c.

B. I. 387.

Akenside,—in his admiration of the Deity,—was an ardent and decided enemy to every species of superstition. In the MS. notes, attached to his own copy, stands the following alteration.

———— " Nor be the hopes
Which flatter youthful bosoms here appall'd,

———

* Ch. i. sect. 2, 3; ch. ii. sect. 2, 3.

Nor let false terror urge you to renounce
This awful theme of undeceitful good,
And truth eternal. Though th' abhorred threats
Of sacred SUPERSTITION, in the quest
Of that kind pair, constrain her kneeling slave,
To quench, and set at nought the lamp of God
Within his frame:—through deserts, thorns, and mire,
Though forth she led him credulous and dark,
And awed with dubious motion; though at length
Benighted, terrified, afflicted, lost,
She leaves him to converse with cells, and graves,
And shapes of death; to listen all alone,
And by the screaming owl's accursed song,
To watch the dreadful workings of his heart;
Or talk with spectres on eternal woe,
Yet be not you dismay'd. A gentler star
Your lovely search enlightens."

This version is very different from those of the first and second poems; and much superior to both. The passage in the first poem (Book I. 387) is supposed to have been levelled at Dr. YOUNG: and a similar application has been made of a stanza in his *Preface to the Odes.*

" Nor where the boding raven chaunts,
Nor near the owl's unhallow'd haunts,
Will she her cares employ;
But flies from ruins and from tombs,
From Superstition's horrid glooms,
To day-light and to joy."

> " And wake the strong divinity of soul,
>   That conquers chance and fate," &c.   *I. 431.*

In the MS. corrected poem, we are directed to read :

> " Which conquers *change* or fate; or whether *tun'd*
>   *For triumph,* on the summit to proclaim
>   Her toils; *around her brow to twine the wreath*
>   Of *ever-lasting* praise; through future worlds
>   *To follow her interminated way.*"

In the second poem :

> " Which conquers *chance* or fate; or on the *height*
>   *The goal assign'd her, haply* to proclaim
>   *Her triumph; on her brow to place the crown*
>   Of *uncorrupted* praise."

────────────────────────── " As the pearl
Shines in the concave of its azure bed,
And painted shells indent their speckled wreath."
                                        I. 454.

> " Concharumque genus parili ratione videmus
>   Pingere telluris gremium."
>   LUCRETIUS, *De Rer. Nat. II.* 374.

Mrs. Barbauld, in her essay on the poem of Akenside, makes an assertion, very extraordinary for a lady of her talents and observation. " In the Pleasures of Imagination only three similes are to be found; viz. that of Memnon's harp; that of the parhelion; and that of the needles." There are, on the contrary, two in the first book, more than she alludes to ; eight in the second ; and six in the third. There are also ten more in the second poem *.

* B. I. l. 454.   As the pearl, &c.
　　　 l. 582.   As when the Persian, &c.
B. II. l.   15.   As the blunt arrow, &c.
　　 l 141.   Like a storm, &c.
　　 l. 350.   As flame ascends, &c.
　　 l. 412.   Flowed like the dewy lustre, &c.
　　 l. 447.   As watery murmurs, &c.
　　 l. 524.   As when a wolf, &c.
　　 l. 604.   As lightning fires, &c.
　　 l. 663.   Flew like the pictures, &c.
B. III. l.   93.   As the bloom of spring, &c.
　　 l. 355.   Like spring's unfolded blossoms, &c.
　　 l. 427.   As when a cloud, &c.
　　 l. 470.   Like a young conqueror, &c.
　　 l. 517.   So fables tell, &c.
　　 l. 527.   Free as the vital breeze, &c.

In the second poem,

B. I. l. 248.   Like clustered isles, &c.
　　 l. 424.   Like a gem, &c.
　　 l. 678.   As travellers by night, &c.
B. II. l.   40.   Like a welcome rill, &c.
　　 l.   65.   As in a polished mirror, &c.
　　 l. 447.   Like fond pilgrims, &c.
　　 l. 578.   As the young lion, &c.
B. III. l. 441.   Like a fair hand-maid, &c.
B. IV. l.   10.   Like waste of sands, &c.
　　 l. 130.   As earth itself, &c.

——————————— " But more lovely still
Is nature's charm, where to the full consent
Of complicated members, to the bloom
Of colour, and the vital change of growth,
Life's holy flame and piercing sense are given,
And active motion speak the tempered soul."

B. I. l. 464.

Τῶν ὄντων τοίνυν τὰ μὲν, &c.

Max. Tyrius, *Dissert.* xvii.

" Ma più natura ci diletta, e piace
    Se al bel contrasto de' tessuti membri,
    E al lumeggiar d' armonici colori,
    E allo sviluppo de' crescenti germi
    Sacra fiamma di vita, un agil senso
    Vien che s'aggiunga, ed un non pigro moto
    Faccia di ben temprata anima fede."

Mazza, *Lib. I.* 596.

" Mind, Mind, alone, (bear witness, earth and heaven !)
    The living fountains in *itself* contains,
    Of beauteous and sublime."

B. I. v. 481.

See Characteristics, i. 130 ; iii. 205 ; i. 137 ; ii. 440 ; iii. 168, 205 ; ii. 83. *Ed.* 1737, *Akenside.*

The alteration in the second poem is very important.

" He, God most high (bear witness, earth and heaven !)
    The living fountains in *himself* contains,
    Of beauteous and sublime."

B. I. v. 563.

The succeeding passage, beginning with

"THEE, O FATHER! this extent
Of matter," &c.;

Dr. Warton compares with a fine one in Pope's Essay on Man:—

"All are but parts of one stupendous whole,
    Whose body Nature is, and God the soul;
    That, changed through all, and yet in all the same;
    Great in the earth, as in th' ethereal frame;
    Warms in the sun, refreshes in the breeze,
    Glows in the stars, and blossoms in the trees;
    Lives through all life, extends through all extent,
    Spreads undivided, operates unspent;
    Breathes in our soul, informs our mortal part,
    As full, as perfect, in a hair, as heart;
    As full, as perfect, in vile man, that mourns,
    As the rapt seraph, that adores and burns.
    To him no high, no low, no great, no small;
    He fills, he bounds, connects, and equals all."

—————————— "Does this capacious scene,
    With half that kindling majesty, dilate
    Thy strong conception, as when BRUTUS rose,
    Refulgent from the stroke of CÆSAR's fate,
    Amid the crowd of patriots, and his arm
    Aloft extending, like eternal Jove,
    When guilt brings down the thunder, call'd aloud
    On TULLY's name, and shook his crimson steel,
    And bad the father of his country hail!"   *I.* 490.

Dugald Stewart thinks *, that the amplifica-

* Philosophy of the active and moral Powers of Man, vol. i. p. 283.

tion of this scene weakens the effect of the simple
narrative of Cicero.   *Cæsare interfecto—statim
cruentum alti extollens M. Brutus pugionem, Cice-
ronem nominatim exclamavit, atque ei recuperatam
libertatem est gratulatus.—Phil. II. 12.*

Akenside,—with other more exalted sentiments,—
seems to have adopted, from the Greek and Roman
theorists, the very questionable doctrine, that the
act of assassinating a tyrant may be associated—

    " With generous counsels and heroic deeds."

"*Brutus perished untimely,*" says the truly learned
and accomplished Mr. Harris in his Essay concerning Happiness, " *and Cæsar did no more.*   It
was thus, as I remember, not long since, you were
expressing yourself, and yet suppose their fortunes
to have been exactly *parallel,* which would you have
preferred? Would you have been *Cæsar* or *Brutus?*
' Brutus,' replied I, ' beyond all controversy.'   He
asked me, ' why; where was the difference, when
their fortunes, as we now supposed them, were
considered the *same?*'   ' There seems,' said I, ' abstract from their fortunes, something, I know not
what, *intrinsically* preferable in the life and character of Brutus.'   ' If that,' said he, ' be true, then
must we derive it, not from the *success* of his en-

deavours; but from their *truth* and *rectitude*. He had the comfort to be conscious, that his cause was a just one. It was impossible that the other should have any such feeling.' ' I believe,' said I, ' that you have explained it *.' "

In Mr. Harris' Philosophical Arrangements is another passage in the same spirit. " The domination of Cæsar acted upon the imagination of Brutus : that imagination acted upon his love for the republic : that love for the republic acted upon his corporal organs. His hand, in consequence, plunged a dagger into Cæsar ; and, for a time, the republic, which he loved, was restored †. "

For a time, the republic, which he loved, was restored.

Harmodius and Aristogiton assassinated Hipparchus ;—Hippias escaped. Harmodius was seized by the guards and massacred. Aristogiton was put to the torture ; and, in revenge to the guards, for having murdered Harmodius, he accused some of them of being privy to his plot. They were innocent; but being the intimate friends of Hippias, the tyrant ordered them to immediate execution.

Who has not heard of Harmodius and Aristo-

* Works, vol. ii. p. 106, 4to. ed. 1801.
† Works, vol. ii. p. 152.

giton? Who has not breathed with quickness, when young, at the bare mention of their names? Were not their statues erected in the market-place at Athens? and was not that an honour never conferred in that city before? Is there not a ballad still preserved, commemorative of the deed? and do not all boys, in classical schools, get it by heart?

Yet who were Harmodius and Aristogiton? and what was their deed? They were friends; and more than companions of Leona, the courtezan. They assassinated a public enemy; but they assassinated him—not in revenge for an injury to their country—but in the spirit of revenge for a private insult, offered to one of themselves.

Brutus plunged a dagger into Cæsar; and, for a time, the republic was restored. Not for one moment! And to that assassination may be attributed a long series of disasters, terminating in an usurpation, which closed with the destruction of the republic in the first instance, and that of the empire in the second.

The assassination was "*not only a crime, but a fault* *!" Antony predicted the result.

---

* The reader will, doubtless, remember the Duke of Otranto's heartless criticism on the murder of the Duke d'Enghein.

" A curse shall light upon the line of men:
Domestic fury, and fierce civil strife,
Shall cumber all the parts of Italy:
Blood and destruction shall be so in use,
And dreadful objects so familiar,
That mothers shall but smile, when they behold
Their infants quarter'd by the hands of war."

The conspirators made ample provision for the success of their plot against Cæsar; but little or none for restoring the republic to its primitive principles. Their conduct, in fact, was the personification of imbecility.

The motives of Brutus have been strangely overlooked. Cæsar had seduced Cato's sister; kept her in obloquy publicly as his mistress; and bought her a jewel at a price equivalent to fifty thousand pounds *! Who should this mistress be? *The mother of Brutus.* If Brutus could live, as he did, for years in friendship under the same roof with the man, who had seduced his mother, he could never have stabbed the seducer for a public benefit. Public motives can only be entertained by good men.

Dante seems to have regarded Brutus with particular indignation. He even represents him, with

* Suetonius. In vit. Cas. c. 50.

T

his friend Cassius, as standing in the inferior regions on each side of Judas Iscariot.

"Quell' anima lassù ch' ha maggior pena,
  Disse 'l maestro, è GIUDA SCARIOTTO,
  Che 'l capo ha dentro, e fuor le gambe mena.
De gli altri duo, ch' hanno 'l capo di sotto,
  Quei che pende dal nero ceffo, è BRUTO :
  Vedi, come si storce, e non fa motto :
E l' altro e Cassio, che par si membruto."

Dell' Inferno, Cant. 34. 60.

Brawlers for liberty ! What are they but the greatest enemies, public liberty has ? They are double enemies ; for they render her name not only suspected but dreaded.

" *License* they mean, when they cry *Liberty.*"

Milton, by this one sentence, explicitly shows, how well he had watched the spirit of his times, and penetrated the intricacy of human affairs. All men love liberty for themselves ; but few are they, who love liberty for others, as well as for themselves :

" Those, who love her, must first be wise and good."

The love of true liberty *, in fact, is always a characteristic in the formation of a noble mind.

---

* TRUE LIBERTY *is the* FREEDOM *of* NATURE, *chastised and regulated by just laws, operating, with ductility and ease, through every portion of the body politic.*

Every statesman should read Plato's *first Alcibi-
ades;* since it was written with the design of incul-
cating the truth, that neither shipping, nor harbours,
nor fortifications, are of any avail to the happiness
of a state; nor extent of empire, nor multiplicity of
population;—*if Virtue does not form the basis of
manners and policy.*

In reference to a tyranny, it is almost a truism
to remark, that the best method of getting rid of
it,—whether that tyranny is wielded by a despot,
an oligarchy, or a democracy,—is for the more respectable portion of the people to be perpetually on
the watch, firm in resolve, quick in action, united
in object, and faithful to themselves. But to assas-
sinate a tyrant is committing a bad action with the
sure result of substituting one tyrant, or one species
of tyranny, for another; probably far worse than
the one which has been exercised and conquered.

————— " As the candid blush
Of him, who strives with Fortune to be just," &c.
I. v. 505.

These, and several succeeding, as well as preceding, lines, are left out in the second poem; and
yet, perhaps, nothing is superior in didactic poetry.

The poet would, it is probable, not have neglected to preserve them, had he been allowed to finish his undertaking ; though the part of the second poem, where they ought to have appeared, seems to be finished ;—amplified but not improved.

———————

" The graceful tear, that flows from other's woes."

I. v. 506.

Darwin has a transcendent passage :

" Nor gilded pearl, that crested Fortune wears,
Nor gem, that twinkling hangs in beauty's ears ;
Not the bright stars, that night's blue arch adorn,
Nor radiant sun, that gilds the rising morn,
Shine with such lustre, as the *tear, that flows
Down Virtue's manly cheeks for other's woes.*"

———————

————————" Trace the forms
Of atoms, moving with incessant change
Their elemental round," &c.

I. 515.

" At, quoniam supra docui, nihil posse creari
De nihilo, neque, quod genitum est, ad nihil revocari ;
Esse immortali primordia corpore debent,
Dissolvi quo quæque supremo tempore possint,
Materies ut subpeditet rebus reparandis.
Sunt igitur solidâ primordia simplicitate,
Nec ratione queunt aliâ, servata per ævom,
Ex infinito jam tempore res reparare."

De Rerum Natura, lib. I. v. 544.

—————————" While among
The herd of servile minds, her strenuous form,
Indignant, flashes on the patriot's eye,
And through the rolls of memor appeal
To ancient honour."

B. I. v. 558.

Had Akenside ever been, as he once hoped, a member of the House of Commons, he would, doubtless, have occasionally startled the members by sudden appeals to " ancient honour." In the MS. notes we read :

—————————" *Different far*
She starts, indignant, on the patriot's eye
Among the servile herd ; her *nervous hand*
Points as she turns the record, and appeals
To ancient honour *."

---

* If he would try effectually to acquire the real science or taste of life, he would discover, that a right mind, or generous affection, had more beauty and charm than all other symmetries in the world ; and, that a grain of honesty and native worth was of more value than all the adventitious ornaments, estates, or preferments ; for the sake of which some of the better sort so often turn KNAVES: forsaking their principles and quitting their honour and freedom, for a mean, timorous, shifting, state of gaudy servitude.—*Characteristics,* vol. iii. 168.

BOOK THE SECOND.

" When shall the laurel and the vocal strain-
 Resume their honours ? When shall we behold
 The tuneful tongue, the Promethean band
 Aspire to ancient praise ?" ·

B. II. 1.

" E quando il lauro, e le vocali corde
     Il prisco onor ripiglieranno ? E quando
 L'armonica vedrem' aurea favella,
     E la Promotea man dietro l'antica
 Lode agognar ?"——

Mazza.

" Oft as the gloomy NORTH, with iron-swarms,
 Tempestuous pouring from her frozen caves
 Blasted the Italian shore ; and *swept the works
 Of Liberty and Wisdom*, down the gulf
 Of all devouring night."

II. 9.

This is an error of long date : but the fact is,
the GOTHS were not such barbarians to Italy, as
were the Italians themselves :——all liberty and wisdom had long been lost, or they had never in-
vaded the country ; and even Rome itself scarcely
suffered more from the sack of the Vandals (not so

much from that of the Goths), than from the imperial troops in the time of Charles V.

————————

——————"How doubly fair,
When first with fresh-born vigour he inhales
The balmy breeze, and feels the blessed sun
Warm at his bosom from the springs of life
Chasing oppressive damps and languid pain."
B. II. v. 92.

These lines remind us of a beautiful stanza in
Gray's poem on the Pleasures arising from Vicissitude.

"See the wretch, that long has tost
On the thorny bed of pain,
At length repair his vigour lost,
And breathe and walk again;" &c. &c.

Gray told Mr. Mathias, that M. Gresset's "*Epitre
à me sœur, sur ma Convalescence,*" gave him the first
idea of this ode.

————————

——————"Nor ever, yet,
The melting rainbow's vernal tinctured hues," &c.
B. II. 103.

Akenside seems to have remembered a passage
in Rapin :—

"Tunc et cælesti quæ dicitur Iris ab arcu,
Splendebit, flores variata coloribus illis,

Quos pluvia accipiunt adverso nubila sole,
Iridis at species varias, variosque colores
Distinguet, variis pro tempestatibus annus."

Hort. I.

" Whether in wonders of the rolling deep,
Or the rich fruits of all-sustaining earth,
Or fine adjusted springs of LIFE and SENSE,
Ye scan the counsels of their author's hand."

B. II. 132.

LOCKE seems to have thought it possible, that a child might think *in utero ;* and DARWIN goes no small way to confirm the conjecture *.

DESCARTES went farther ; for he carried his imaginative powers so far as to suppose, that the soul, when it enters the body, is informed with the whole series of metaphysical notions ; that it possesses all abstract ideas ; that it even knows God ; and has the power of comprehending infinite space !

All this Descartes seems to have thought not only possible, but probable ; but he thought, at the same time, that these sublime truths the soul forgets at the moment, in which it beholds—as Madame de Stael would, probably, say on such an occasion—" *Aurore d'une vie nouvelle.*"

Let us hazard a conjecture.

* Temple of Nature, Cant. III. l. 144. *in notis.*

The pistils of some flowers produce seeds, without receiving any pollen from the stamens; and birds produce eggs without any communication *cum maritis*. But those seeds, if planted, will never vegetate; nor will those eggs produce the germ of a living chicken. Most fishes, and some reptiles, have no communication *cum maritis* whatever. They shed, and *mariti* fertilize afterwards.

From these phenomena it would appear, that the materials, forming the body of the future plant, bird, fish, and reptile, are secreted *in feminis;* and the living spirit *in masculis*. How the bodily machine acquires existence in the one, and how the principle of life is secreted in the other, are both secrets alike.

May not this be applied to the human subject?

The *pater* having communicated the living principle to the inactive and unconscious mass (existent in *matrice*), the latter becomes a mansion for the former to reside in.

Through the windows of this mansion (viz. the SENSES), the living principle receives impressions from the external universe, which engender what are called IDEAS; and the capacity of receiving those ideas is what may be called MIND.

> " Passion's fierce illapse
> Rouses the mind's whole fabric; with supplies
> Of daily impulse keeps the elastic powers
> Intensely pois'd, and polishes anew,
> By that collision, all the fine machine;" &c.
>
> *B. II. v.* 158.

This passage is thus rendered by the Italian translator, who illustrates the subject with a passage from Pope *.

> ——————————— " Questa col fiero
> Urto per tutta l'anima s'interna;
> E col soccorso de' frequenti impulsi
> Agevola, distende, e ognor mantiene
> L'elastiche potenze equilibrate;
> E in questa poi *collision*, più tersa
> Tutta la fina macchina diviene."
>
> *Libro Secondo,* 199.

In respect to the foundation of the mysterious kind of pleasure†, which is sometimes experienced in the exercise of the passions, generally regarded as

---

* " But strength of mind is exercise; not rest.
    The rising tempest puts in act the soul;
    Parts it may ravage, but preserves the whole."
        Pope. *Sag. sopra l'Uomo, Ep.* ii. *v.* 104.

† *B. II.* 157, 693.

painful, Akenside dismisses the solution of LUCRE-
TIUS *, and adopts that of DU Bos † ; viz. *that it*
arises from the general delight, which the mind
tastes in its own activity; and its abhorrence of a
state of indolence, joined with the self-applause,
which always attends the emotion, when natural
and just.

This solution, however, is not more strictly
accordant with true science, than that of Lucretius :
it is even less so : for it is, assuredly, more natural to
ascribe the sensation, alluded to, to a feeling of
conscious safety, than to one of conscious activity.

It seems, however, as if it would be more con-

---

* " Suave, mari magno turbantibus æquora ventis,
    E terrâ magnum alterius spectare laborem :
    Non, quia vexari quemquam est *jocunda voluptas,*
    Sed, quibus ipse malis careas, quia cernere suave est."
                    LUCRET. *De Rer. Natur.* ii. 1.

Beattie has an admirable passage:

" And oft the craggy cliff he loved to climb,
    When all in mist the world below was lost.
    What *dreadful pleasure* ‡ ! There to stand sublime,
    Like ship-wreck'd mariner on desert coast."
                    Minstrel, i. *st.* 21.

† Reflexions critiques sur la Poesie et sur la Peinture.

---

‡ How far superior to the *jocunda voluptas* of Lucretius !

sonant with truth, were we to reduce its solution to that one simple canon, which teaches that misfortune is attractive, and thence elicits sympathy much after the manner, that magnets affine and planets gravitate.

" 'Twas in the windings of an ancient wood," &c.
B. II. 187.

See Leibnitz, Essais de Theodicée, sur la Bonté de Dieu, la Liberté de l'Homme, et l'Origine du Mal, i. 21. 209.   Moral, Physique, Metaphysique, 118, 119, 209, 241.

The purport of Akenside's allegory is to solve the difficulty, in respect to the origin of evil : it must, however, be confessed, that there is an obscurity throughout ;—yet if he fail,—we are to consider, that he fails in a point, in which it was impossible to succeed.   The subject is invincible !

———————— " Is thy short span
Capacious of this universal frame ?
Thy wisdom all-sufficient* ?   Thou—alas !
Dost thou aspire to judge between the Lord
Of Nature and his works ?"
B. II. l. 245.

The last two lines remind us of two well-known verses in the book of Job.

* Commanding.—*MS.*

——————— " 'Twas a horrid pile
Of hills, with many a shaggy forest mix'd,
With many a sable cliff and glittering stream
Aloft recumbent."

B. II. l. 274.

In the *MS.* notations we are desired to read—

——————— " 'Twas a horrid pile
Of *cliffs*, with many a shaggy forest mix'd,
With many a sable *heath*, and glittering stream
Aloft *incumbent.*"

———————

" Remurmuring rush'd the congregated floods
With hoarser inundation."

B. II. 282, 3.

" *More ponderous* rush'd the congregated floods,
And louder still resounded."

MS. Notation.

In respect to this and to other MS. corrections, Mr. Pinkerton says:—" *As I know that Akenside's work on the Pleasures of Imagination is deservedly one of your most favourite poems, I send you inclosed what, I have no doubt, you will set a due value upon: no less than a copy of all the corrections he made with his own hand on that poem. They were inserted in the margin of his printed copy, which afterwards passed into the hands of a

* Heron's Letters.

gentleman, from a friend of whom, and of my own, a very ingenious young Templar, I received them. At what time they were written I cannot pretend to say; much less to reveal the author's reasons for not giving an edition according to them. You will observe, that a few of them have been adopted by the author in his proposed alteration of the poem; as appears from the two books, and part of the third, of that alteration, published by Mr. Dyson in his edition of Akenside's poems, 1772, 4to., but far the greater part is unpublished*; and that the most valuable, as being evidently written ere the author had taken up the strange idea, that *poetry was only perfect oratory.* So that I will venture to say, that an edition of the Pleasures of Imagination, adopting most of these corrections, would be the most perfect, ever yet known†."

——————————————————————"With full accord
Answering the mighty model, he had chosen,
The best and fairest of unnumbered worlds,
That lay from everlasting in the store
Of his divine conceptions."

B. II. l. 333.

---

* And these only it has been thought proper to insert.
† An edition, combining these and other advantages, will, probably, be published at no very distant period.

" This opinion," says Akenside, " is so old, that Timæus Locrus calls the Supreme Being δαμιϱυγὸς τῶ Βαλτίονος, *the artificer of that which is best ;* and represents him as resolving in the beginning to produce the most excellent work, and as copying the world most exactly from his own intelligible and essential idea; *so that it yet remains, as it was at first, perfect in beauty, and will never stand in need of any correction or improvement.* See the vision at the end of the *Theodicée of Leibnitz.*"

Surely this is begging the question in a very strange and contracted manner. Who can suppose this world, in which evil must be acknowledged to exist *, to be the *lest that the Deity was capable of forming?* This is a subject beyond our comprehension; but men differ greatly upon it.

Some years since I travelled, for several days, with a Venetian gentleman, who had lost all his patrimony during the occupation of Venice by the French. We got out of the coach near the village of Llandisilio, and passing through the church-

---

* Who can refuse to believe that EVIL exists, while the bodies, even of good men, are liable to the pangs of

" Intestine stone and ulcer, colic-pangs,
  Demoniac frenzy, moping melancholy,
  And moon-struck madness, pining atrophy,
  Marasmus, and wide-wasting pestilence?"

yard, we sat down upon one of the grave-stones; and the conversation having taken a serious turn— " This is indeed a beautiful valley !" said he, " and the country we have passed through is, I think, almost equal to any thing I have seen in the Venetian states.   But what avails all this beauty ? Where man places his foot, the box of Pandora bursts open.   Indeed, to me it appears as if the Being, who created the globe, left it before he had brought his plan to maturity, and passed on to call forth new creations, more conformable to the impresses, existing in his own mind.   We are the dregs of the universe !"

This was the momentary error of despondency : but none are more ignorantly presumptuous than those, who would set limits to the capabilities of " *the unfathomable deep*."

Not only BINARY and TERNARY systems have been traced in the heavens, but QUADRUPLE, QUINTUPLE, and MULTIPLE ones; all connected in systems of reciprocal attraction.   Even their periods of revolution have, in some instances, been detected. One, for instance, in the SERPENT, occupying 375 years; a second in the VIRGIN, 708 years; a third in Leo, 1200 years; and a fourth in Bootes occupying 1681 years !

To doubt that these, and all other SUNS, COMETS, PLANETS and SATELLITES, are peopled with intelligent Beings, is to have a very limited conception of the uses, extension, splendour, and magnificence of the universe, indeed; as well as of the sublimity of operation, characteristic of the SOVEREIGN POWER.

The ELECTRIC FLUID is a substance; every particle of LIGHT is a substance; the ESSENCE OF ATTRACTION is a substance. All these fluids are passing and repassing, in myriads of directions, in every fractional moment of time. There is, in fact, no interval. There is a communication, then, every instant,—one stellar body with another.

The SOUL of MAN is not of earthly substance, but— speaking figuratively*—of etherial substance. * * * All fluids are VEHICLES. * * * * May not the soul of man, at the period in which it separates from the body, be conveyed on one, or all of these Vehicles combined? * * * WHITHER? * * *

" Wait the great teacher, Death, and God adore."

———————— " Looking up, I view'd
A vast, gigantic, spectre, striding on,

---

* We can only speak figuratively, on a subject of this kind.

Through murmuring thunder, and a waste of clouds,
With dreadful action !   Black as night, his brow
Relentless frowns involv'd:—his savage limbs,
With sharp impatience, violent he writh'd,
As through convulsive anguish ; and his hand,
Arm'd with a scorpion lash, full oft he rais'd,
In madness, to his bosom ; while his eyes
Rain'd bitter tears, and bellowing loud, he shook
The void with horror.—Silent, by his side,
The virgin came ; no discomposure stirr'd
Her features: from the glooms, which hung around,
No stain of darkness, mingled with the beam
Of her divine effulgence."

                                 B. II. v. 506—520.

This whole passage is an instance of the true sublime ; and the picture may be associated with that of Death and Sin in Milton's Paradise Lost.

————————————— " Ask the faithful youth*,
Why the cold urn of her he fondly loved,
So often fills his arms," &c.   *B. II.* 683.

---

* Chiedi al fido Garzon, perché si spesso
Abbracci e stringa di colei, che tanto
Ebbe de' suoi sospir, la gelid' urna ;
O perché sciolga solitario il piede
A lei recando nelle tacite ore
Delle lagrime sue mesto tributo.
Ah ! ti dirà, quanti ha tesori il mondo,
Questa non mi farian' ora si sacra
Unqua obbliar, in cui lungi alle cure
Del livor, del tumulto, una gradita

That Akenside was alive to all the soft impulses of nature, we have already shown. The loss of Parthenia he seems never to have forgotten ; and the grief, he had anticipated in the days of his youth, he was fated to experience in the season of manhood.

—————————— " When the pious band
Of youths, who fought for freedom and their sires
Lay side by side in gore."

B. II. 726.

Rimembranza mi tragge, e'l core efflitto
Coi dolci sguardi di virtù lusinga,
E in estasi converte il pianto mio.

MAZZA.

In reference to this passage it has been observed, that " when the mind has been liberally and elegantly cultivated; where much sensibility and strength of passion are present, and the misfortunes occurring turn upon the loss of some tender and beloved connexion ; in this case, what may be called the luxury of grief is more fully and exquisitely displayed. That mild and gentle sorrow, which, in the bosom of the good and of the feeling, succeeds the strong energies of grief, is of a nature so soothing and grateful, so friendly to the soft emotions of the soul, that those, whose friendship or whose love, the hand of fate has severed, delight in the indulgence of reflections, which lead to past endearment, which, dwelling on the virtues, the perfections of the dead, breathe the pure spirit of melancholy enthusiasm."—*Drake*

" The reader will here naturally recollect the fate of the second battalion of Thebes, which at the battle of Cheronéa, was utterly destroyed; every man being found dead by the side of his friend. This affecting circumstance is recorded by Plutarch, in his life of Pelopidas."—AKENSIDE.

————————— " When honoured *urns*
Of patriots and of chiefs,—the awful *bust*
And *storied* arch, to glut the coward rage
Of regal envy, strew the public way
With hallowed ruins."

B. II. 734.

To this passage may be traced Gray's line:—

" Can *storied urn,* or animated *bust?*"

and to the following, perhaps, Johnson's still more celebrated one of—

" And panting time toil'd after him in vain."

————————— " To eyes, to ears,
To every organ of the copious mind
He offereth all his treasures.   Him the hours;
The seasons him obey; and changeful TIME
Sees him, at will, keep measure with his flight,
At will outstrip it."

B. IV. v. 109.

BOOK THE THIRD.

———————————————"The spacious west,
And all the teeming regions of the south,
Hold not a quarry to the curious flight
Of knowledge, half so tempting and so fair
As MAN to MAN."

B. III. v. 7.

Pope says

"The proper study of mankind is man."

Akenside was fully aware of this axiom, and wrote his poem to confirm the truth of it : and yet it is very remarkable, that he omitted it in his second poem. It is not impossible, however, that he might have intended to insert it in some other portion of the part, he meditated. It is thus rendered by MAZZA:

"Il diffuso occidente, e le feraci
    Australi region certo non hanno
    Minieri si mirabile, e che tanto
    Aletti del Saper l'avido volo,
    Quanto l'Uomo dell' Uom merta i riflessi *."

---

* From the manner in which this passage, and indeed the whole poem, has been translated, how can a French reader

——————" Where the powers
Of Fancy neither lessen nor enlarge
The images of things," &c.

B. III. l. 18.

Diogenes Laertius, lib. vii. ; Meditations of M. Aurelius ; and the Discourses of Epictetus ; Arrian, lib. i. c. 12., and lib. ii. c. 22. See also Characteristics, vol. i. from p. 313 to 321.—AKENSIDE.

————————" Some elate
With martial splendour," &c.

B. III. v. 98.

This picture reminds us of certain parts of Othello's apology ; and serves to show the wide difference between the impudence and modesty of valour. Akenside's description is, in fact, a reversion of that, sketched by Shakspeare.

" He stalks, resounding in magnific phrase
The vanity of riches, the contempt
Of pomp and power."

B. III. v. 136.

have even the smallest conception of that exquisite harmony of rhythmus, which distinguishes the original ?

" *Les vastes contrées de l'occident, les fecondes régions du midi n'offrent rien de si digne de recherches, rien qui mérite autant l'examen de la Science, que l'homme ne mérite l'étude de l'homme.*"

This picture is from Lucian; though I cannot refer to the page or subject. Seneca, who was rich, and yet a contemner of wealth, may be supposed to have sat for the original portrait of him,

> " Whose eye regards not his illustrious pomp
> And ample store; but as indulgent streams
> To cheer the barren soil, and spread the fruits
> Of joy."

v. 147.

" Mark the sable woods," &c.
B. III. l. 286.

In respect to lawgivers, Akenside seems to have given a decided preference to MINOS, SOLON, and NUMA. He does not once mention LYCURGUS. Nearly the whole of the third book of the second poem is devoted to the history of Solon; and a fine scene from nature is rendered much more affecting to the mental eye by the poet's having associated with it two of the most celebrated legislators of antiquity.

> ————————" Mark the sable woods,
> That shade sublime yon mountain's nodding brow;
> With what religious awe the solemn scene
> Commands your steps! as if the reverend form

Of MINOS or of NUMA should forsake
Th' Elysian seats, and, down th' embowering shade,
Move to your pausing eye."

I am indebted to Mr. Alison's work on the Nature
of the Emotions of Sublimity and Beauty * for the
first appreciation of this circumstance †.

---

* Pages 19, 20, 21.

† " There is also a passage in the same poet's Ode to Suspicion," he goes on to observe, " in which a scene, which is,
in general, only beautiful, is rendered strikingly sublime,
from the imagery with which it is connected.

    ' 'Tis thus to work her baneful power,
      SUSPICION waits the sullen hour
         Of fretfulness and strife ;
    When care the infirmer bosom wrings,
    Or Eurus waves his murky wings
         To damp the seats of life.

    But come ! forsake the scene unblest,
    Which first beheld your faithful breast
         To groundless fears a prey ;
    Come where, with my prevailing lyre,
    The skies, the streams, the groves, conspire
         To charm your doubts away.

    Throned in the sun's descending car,
    What power, unseen, diffuseth far
         This tenderness of mind ?
    What Genius smiles in yonder flood ?
    What God, in whispers from the wood,
         Bids every thought be kind ?' "

" 'Twas thus, if ancient Fame the truth unfold,
 Two faithful needles, from th' informing touch
 Of the same parent stone, together drew
 Its mystic virtue; and at first conspired,
 With fatal impulse, quivering to the pole.
 Then, though disjoin'd by kingdoms, though the main
 Roll'd its broad surge betwixt, and different stars
 Beheld their wakeful motions, yet preserved
 The former friendship, and remember'd still
 Th' alliance of their birth: whate'er the line
 Which one possess'd, nor pause, nor quiet knew
 The sure associate, ere with trembling speed
 He found its path, and fix'd unerring there."

B. III. 325—337.

As Akenside directs us to the poem, recited by
Cardinal Bembo, in the character of Lucretius, in
Strada's Prolusions, the reader will not be dis-
pleased to find it here.

" Magnesi genus est lapidis mirabile, cui si
Corpora ferri plura, stylosve admoveris; inde
Non modo vim, motumque trahent, quo semper ad ursam,
Qua lucet vicina polo se vertere tentent:
Verum etiam mira inter se ratione modoque
Quotquot cum lapidem tetigêre styli, simul omnes
Conspirare situm motumque videbis in unum,
Ut si forte ex his aliquis Roma moveatur,
Alter ad hunc motum, quamvis sit dissitus longè
Arcano se naturai fædere vertat.
  Ergo age, si quid scire voles, qui distat, amicum,
Ad quem nulla accedere possit epistola; sume
Planum orbem patulumque, notas elementaque prima

Ordine, quo discunt pueri describe per oras
Extremas orbis; medioque repone jacentem,
Qui tetigit magneta, stylum; ut versatilis inde
Literulam quamcunque velis, contingere possit.
Hujus ad exemplum, simili fabrica veris orbem
Margine descriptum, munitumque indice ferri,
Ferri quod motum magnete accepit ab illo.
Hunc orbem discessurus sibi portet amicus,
Conveniatque priùs, quo tempore, queisve diebus
Exploret, stylus an trepidet, quidve indice signet.
   His ita compositis, si clam cupis alloqui amicum,
Quem procul a tete terrai distinet ora;
Orbi adjunge manum, ferrum versatile tracta.
Hic dispôsta vides elementa in margine toto:
Quies opus est ad verba notis, huc dirige ferrum;
Literulasque, modò hanc, modò et silam cuspide tange,
Dum ferrum per eas iterumque iterumque rotando,
Componas sigillatim sensa omnia mentis.
Mira fides longè qui distat cernit amicus
Nullius impulsu trepidare volubile ferrum,
Nunc huc, nunc illuc discurrere: conscius hæret,
Observatque styli ductum, sequiturque legendo
Hinc atque hinc elementa, quibus in verba coactis
Quid sit opus sentit, ferroque interprete discit.
Quin etiam cum stare stylum videt, ipse vicissim
Si qua respondenda putet simili ratione
Literulis variè tactis, rescribit amico.
   O utinam hæc ratio scribendi prodeat usu:
Cautior, et citior properaret epistola, nullas
Latronum verita insidias, fluviosque morantes.
Ipse suis Princeps manibus sibi conficeret rem;
Nos soboles scribarum emersi ex æquore nigro,
CONSECRAREMUS CALAMUM MAGNETIS AD ORAS."

STRADA. Prol. Lib. II. Prol. VI.

" ———— By degrees the mind
Feels her young nerves dilate : the plastic powers
Labour for action : blind emotions heave
His bosom, and with holiest *frenzy* * caught,
From earth to heaven, he rolls his daring eye,
From heaven to earth."

B. III. l. 380.

Thus Shakspeare :—

" The poet's eye, in a fine frenzy rolling,
Glances from earth to heaven, from heaven to earth,
And as imagination," &c.

———————

" ———— As when a cloud
Of gathering hail with limpid crusts of ice
Enclosed, and obvious to the beaming sun,
Collects his large effulgence, straight, the heavens
With equal flames present on either hand
The radiant visage; PERSIA stands at gaze
Appall'd; and on the brink of GANGES doubts
The snowy vested seer, in Mithra's name,
To which the fragrance of the south shall burn,
To which his warbled orisons ascend."

B. III. v. 427.

This very sublime simile stands a chance of not
being exactly understood by some readers; but

* In the MS. corrected poem we are directed to read:
" ———— with *holiest* frenzy caught
From earth to heaven, he *darts his searching eye*
From heaven to earth."

when they are reminded, that Akenside alludes to
the two suns, one real, the other fictitious, so often
beheld in very hot, as well as in very cold, tem-
peratures, the sublimity will be so striking, that a
critic, perhaps, might be justified in placing it in a
rank, second only to Milton's simile of Satan to the
Sun during the time of an eclipse.

" —— a visionary Paradise disclosed,
    Amid the dubious wild," &c.

                                    B. III. v. 511.

This whole passage seems to have been founded
on the following description in the Spectator, No.
413. "*We are every where entertained with pleasing
shows and apparitions, we discover imaginary glo-
ries in the heavens and in the earth, and see some
of this visionary beauty poured out upon the whole
creation. But what a rough unsightly sketch of
nature should we be entertained with, did all her
colouring disappear, and the several distinctions of
light and shade vanish! In short, our souls are,
at present, delightfully lost and bewildered in a
pleasing delusion; and we walk about like the en-
chanted hero in a romance, who sees beautiful cas-
tles, woods and meadows, at the same time hears the
warbling of birds and purling of streams; but upon*

the finishing of some secret spell, the fantastic scene breaks up, and the disconsolate knight finds himself on a barren heath, or in a solitary forest."

" What then is TASTE ?"

B. III. v. 515.

Akenside here traces the causes to which may be referred the pleasure, which is received from all, that strikes us in the material world with the sensation of beauty.   These are traced to the conclusion, that " *the beauty and sublimity of the qualities of matter arise from their being the signs or expressions of such qualities, as are fitted by the constitution of our nature, to produce emotion.*"   The passage is thus rendered by the Italian translator.

" Dunque il Gusto ch' è mai, se non l'interne
 Potenze agili e forti, e a sentir pronte
 Ogn' impulso leggiero ? un retto senso
 Il Decente a discernere, e' l Sublime,
 E in ogni spezie a ripulsar ben presto
 Deformi obbietti, inordinati e rozzi ?
 Questo prestar non pon gemme, o tesori,
 Di porpora splendor, industria ; e solo
 Dio solo, allor che l'efficace destra
 La secreta dell' alme indole impronta,
 Egli può sol l'Omnipossente Padre
 Prudente, giusto, libero, siccome
 L'aura dì vita e la luce del Cielo,
 Le bellezze svelar della Natura."

See BETTINELLI's *Dell' Entusiasmo delle bell'
Arti.* This work is very little known in this country; and yet it is worthy of being so. The author
seems to have been acquainted with Milton, Ossian,
and other British writers; but I do not remember his having once alluded to Akenside; a circumstance, rather extraordinary, when we consider
the nature of his work.

————————

——————— " Ask the SWAIN,
Who journeys homeward from a summer day's
Long labour," &c.
                              B. III. v. 526.

Beattie has a fine passage, in some degree associating with this:

" From silent mountains, straight with startling sound,
    Torrents are hurl'd; green hills emerge; and lo,
The trees with foliage, cliffs with flowers are crown'd;
    Pure rills through vales of verdure warbling go,
And wonder, love, and joy, the PEASANT's heart o'erflow."

————————

" Amid the mighty uproar, while below
    The nations tremble, SHAKSPEARE looks abroad,
From some high cliff superior, and enjoys
    The elemental war."
                              B. III. v. 555.

" Horace regards it as the last effort of philosophic fortitude to behold, without terror and amazement, this immense and glorious fabric of the universe :—

> ' Hunc solem, et stellas, et decedentia certis
> Tempora momentis, sunt qui formidine nulla
> Imbuti spectant.'

" Lucretius is a poet not to be suspected of giving way to superstitious terrors ; yet when he supposes the whole mechanism of Nature laid open by the master of his philosophy, his transport on this magnificent view, which he has represented in the colours of such bold and lively poetry, is overcast with a shade of secret dread and horror :—

> ' His tibi me rebus quædam divina voluptas
> Percipit, atque horror, quod sic natura tua vi
> Tam manifesta patet ex omni parte retecta.' "

BROWN.

> " Oh, blest of Heav'n ! whom not the languid songs
> Of Luxury, the Siren !" &c.

B. III. l. 568.

Shaftesbury's ideas on luxury are stated in vols. i. 310. 315. 319, &c. ; ii. 147, &c. ; iii. 199. 304. His ideas in regard to pleasure may be traced in i. 308 ; ii. 226 ; iii. 200. 229. He proves, that pleasure has no rule of good, i. 309. 339 : that the pleasures of mind are far superior to those of the body, ii. 99, 100: and that even men of pleasure are compelled to acknowledge the influence and delights, which impregnate a virtuous bosom, i. 140. Ed. 1737.

———————

——————— " Not a breeze
Flies o'er the meadow," &c.

III. 593.

Marcus Antoninus, lib. iii. 2.—AKENSIDE.

———————

——————— " What though not all
Of mortal offspring," &c.

The advantages of a cultivated imagination are here set forth in a very masterly manner.

——————— " What though not all
Of mortal offspring can attain the heights
Of envied life; though only few possess
Patrician treasures or imperial state;
Yet Nature's care, to all her children just,
With richer treasures and an ampler state,
Endows at large whatever happy man
Will deign to use them.

                        His the city's pomp,
The rural honours his.   Whate'er adorns
The princely dome, the column and the arch,
The breathing marbles and the sculptur'd gold,
Beyond the proud possessor's narrow claim,
His tuneful breast enjoys.

> For him the spring
> Distils her dews, and from the silken gem
> Its lucid leaves unfolds: for him the hand
> Of autumn tinges every fertile branch
> With blooming gold and blushes like the morn.
> Each passing hour sheds tribute from her wings;
> And still new beauties meet his lonely walk,
> And loves unfelt attract him. Not a breeze
> Flies o'er the meadow, not a cloud imbibes
> The setting sun's effulgence, not a strain
> From all the tenants of the warbling shade
> Ascends, but whence his bosom can partake
> Fresh pleasure unreproved*."

---

* Professor Stuart has a beautiful observation in his Philosophical Essays. (P. 509. 4to.) " When a man has succeeded, at length, in cultivating his imagination, things, the most familiar and unnoticed, disclose charms invisible before. The same objects and events, which were lately beheld with indifference, occupy now all the powers and capacities of the soul; the contrast between the present and the past serving only to enhance and to endear so unlooked for an acquisition. What Gray has so finely said of the pleasures of vicissitude, conveys but a faint image of what is experienced by the man, who after having lost, in vulgar occupation and vulgar amusement, his earliest and most precious years, is thus introduced, at last, to a new heaven and a new earth.

> The meanest floweret of the vale,
> The simplest note that swells the gale,
> The common sun, the air, the skies,
> To him are opening paradise."

x

——————— " With God himself hold converse."
                                    B..III. 629.

There is an elegant paper in the Tatler (or Spectator), by BISHOP BERKELEY; the moral of which is, that he cared little to be the real possessor of an estate, as long as he was allowed the use and pleasure of walking over it, as often as he pleased. Akenside alludes to this in a line quoted above.

" Beyond the proud possessor's narrow claim."

Akenside was doomed to the dust and poison of a large city, during the greatest portion of his life. His proper sphere was the garden and the valley, the mountain, the ocean, and the firmament, where with a hallowed mind he might have

————————— " With God himself
Held converse, grew familiar, day by day,
With his conceptions, acted on his plan,
And form'd to his the relish of his soul*.

————————— * " L'Uomo in tal guisa,
Cui dilettano l'opre di Natura,
Con Dio conversa, e all' alte idee di Lui
Di giorno in giorno familiar si rende;
Ed operando sul modello istesso
I suoi disegna su i piacer di Dio."

                                    MAZZA.

Johnson, in criticising this poem, cites a passage from Mr. Walker. "Akenside's picture of man is grand and beautiful, but unfinished. The immortality of the soul, which is the natural consequence of the appetites and powers she is invested with, is scarcely once hinted throughout the poem." In apology for which supposed omission, Johnson concedes, that he has omitted what was not properly in his plan.

This is a very striking instance to prove, I think, that Mr. Walker could have known as little of this poem as Johnson himself; neither of them having, it is more than probable, read it with the confined attention, necessary to embrace the whole of its subjects.

Akenside's poem would have been very defective indeed, had the author (by omission) stript man of the high destiny for which his virtues will endow him at the period of death. But he has not done so; the following passages all implying, and that most expressly, this all-commanding consummation :—

> —————"While the voice
> Of truth and virtue up the steep ascent
> Of Nature calls him to his high reward,
> Th' applauding smile of heaven," &c.

B. I. 163.

x 2

——————————" The high-born soul
Disdains to rest her heav'n-aspiring wing
Beneath its native quarry."

B. I. 183.

——————————" For from the birth
Of mortal man, the Sovereign Maker said,
That not in humble, or in brief delight,"

 * *   *   *   *

——————————" But from these,
Turning, disdainful, to an equal good,
Through all th' ascent of things enlarge his view,
Till every bound, at length, should disappear,
And infinite Perfection close the scene."

B. I. l. 212. *Second Poem.*

" To trace her hallow'd light through future worlds,
And bless Heav'n's image in the heart of man."

B. I. 436.

——————————" The generous glebe,

 •   *   •   *   •

Are only pledges of a state sincere,
Th' integrity and order of their frame,
When all is well within, and every end
Accomplish'd."

B. I. 364.

" Led by that hope sublime, whose cloudless eye,
Through the fair toils and ornaments of earth,
Discerns the nobler life, reserved for heaven."

Second Poem, l. 489.

————" Beyond the adamantine gates
Of death expatiates; as his birthright claims
Inheritance in all the works of God;
Prepares for endless time his plan of life,
And counts the universe itself its home."

B. II. l. 147.

————" Nor is the care of Heaven withheld,
From granting to the task proportion'd aid,
That, in their stations, all may persevere
To climb th' ascent of being, and approach
For ever nearer to the life divine *."

B. II. l. 359.

And here we may triumphantly cite a passage,—
forming a comprehensive and decisive antidote to
the puerile and pestilential arguments of atheism;—
than which nothing, perhaps, in human language
can be quoted more harmonious in point of taste;
more strictly accordant with true ethics; or more
beautiful or sublime in poetry and philosophy.

"Lo! she appeals to Nature; to the winds
And rolling waves,—the sun's unwearied course,—

---

* Shaftesbury, also, clearly admits a future state; witness
those passages in his Characteristics, where he argues not
only on its probability, but its absolute necessity and proof:
vol. ii. 275. See also, i. 18, 97, 98—102; ii. 236, 7; iii. 303;
as well as his opinions in respect to rewards and punishments, ii. 65, 273; i. 97; ii. 69; i. 100.

> The elements and seasons.   ALL declare
> For what the ETERNAL MAKER has ordain'd
> The powers of Man.   We feel within ourselves
> His energy divine ;   HE tells the heart,
> HE meant, HE made us, to behold and love
> What HE beholds and loves, the gen'ral orb
> Of life and being ; to be great like HIM,
> Beneficent and active.
>   Thus the men,
> Whom Nature's works can charm, with God himself
> Hold converse, grow familiar, day by day,
> With his conceptions, act upon his plan,
> And form to HIS the relish of their souls."
>
> *B. III. v.* 620.

The Deity, and a future life, are the highest subjects, that can engage the exercise of the human imagination.

ARISTOTLE associates the mind of man with a tablet, on which there is no picture ; HOOKER compares it to a book, wherein nothing is yet written ; but in which all things may be written ; and to these similitudes may be traced LOCKE's celebrated illustration, in regard to *" white paper."*

Man, then, is born, not in sin and impurity ; but in purity and innocence ; susceptible of all good thoughts, and comprehensively capacious of all virtuous deeds.

The true object of education is not to enable us to play, more cunningly than others, " the subtle *game*" of life; but to give us judgment to perceive the true objects of existence; wisdom to preserve a rectitude of path; and pure mental associations, wherewith to charm us to our journey's end.

Shall the hours of our youth, then, always be wasted? Shall the fountains of our imagination always be poisoned? and shall the science of society always be as dark as the Sibyl, and as difficult as the Calculus?

Are these the hopes for which we live? Are these the fruits for which we toil? Are these the ends for which we suffer?

The GENIUS of EDUCATION still rests, as it were, with one foot in his cradle. He stands, contemplating the sublime volume of human happiness; but till he presents the leaf, imparting to governments the duty of teaching MEN the *apparently* contrasted arts of enlarging their minds, contracting their wants, regulating their wishes *, and referring all to one stu-

---

* The practice of the past and of the present has been, and still is, in decided opposition to this; and ever will be so, until Political Economists shall have discovered the true object for which governments are established; viz. not for the purpose of making nations rich, vain, powerful and imperious; but content with little, and *practically* desirous of promoting the comfort of all that breathe.

As no one comes into the world through the medium of his

pendous cause;—instead of ease after mild labour,
and thoughts, on which the mind, contented, may
repose; for the RICH and GREAT, little better will
there be than abundance and languor, proud hopes,
ambitious aspirations, heartless deeds, and sleepless
nights: for the POOR, intensity of labour and intensity of want; impurity and disease; sorrow and
ignominy; hopeless honesty, and cruel wounds.

own choice, every one, that does come, has a natural right,—
until that right is forfeited by the infringement of good laws,
—not only to *food* and *clothing*, but to *a life, valuable to
himself.*

When these cannot be commanded by honest endeavours
(of body or of mind), the state of society is cruelly, if not
criminally, defective; and it becomes the imperative duty
of all to aid an existing government in putting forth its full
extent of lawful influence and power, to the end, that the
LEGITIMATE RIGHT may command the LEGITIMATE RESULT.

THE END.

LONDON:
PRINTED BY THOMAS DAVISON, WHITEFRIARS.